HELEN FREEMAN

Starting out as a professional actress, Helen Freeman's career evolved to include teaching – in the classroom, with her own workshop company specialising in Shakespeare, and through her one-woman show about Anne Hathaway.

She has extensive experience of the audition process as an audition panellist, student-performance assessor and teacher at the Guildford School of Acting – and as a parent, going through the whole audition process with her son, who trained as an actor.

SO YOU WANT TO
GO TO DRAMA SCHOOL?

*A guide for young people
who want to train as actors*

Helen Freeman

NICK HERN BOOKS
London
www.nickhernbooks.co.uk

A Nick Hern Book

SO YOU WANT TO GO TO DRAMA SCHOOL?
first published in Great Britain in 2010
by Nick Hern Books Limited
The Glasshouse, 49a Goldhawk Road, London W12 8QP

Reprinted with revisions in 2019

Cover designed by Peter Bennett

Typeset by Nick Hern Books, London
Printed and bound in Great Britain by
Ashford Colour Press, Gosport, Hampshire

A CIP catalogue record for this book
is available from the British Library

ISBN 978 1 84842 016 8

FSC
www.fsc.org

MIX
Paper from
responsible sources
FSC® C011748

This book is dedicated to actors everywhere

Contents

Appendices

Introduction

The large number of reality 'star-maker' shows that appear regularly on our television screens have all served to foster the dreams and aspirations of many would-be stars of stage and screen. Ironically, the very small number of successes on stage and screen seem also to give hope to each and every one who would like to be the 'next big thing'.

This book aims to give honest, straightforward advice. It aims to help students make the decisions and prepare to train for their careers. It is not, however, a manual for acting, to be followed step by step like a recipe book. Rather, it is designed to encourage commitment and independence of thought and to stimulate students towards their goals; in other words, to get them to be *proactive and thinking for themselves*. From this will come a self-awareness, self-evaluation and self-improvement which will continue into and beyond their formal training. This vital preparation cannot wait until school is only a memory. This book is addressed, in the main part, directly to these students.

It is also designed to give practical and accessible advice to parents and teachers – on training, training establishments and the kind of preparation that should be undertaken – who can often feel adrift in uncharted waters when their child or student declares that they want to be an actor. It scarcely needs pointing out that what this book cannot do is guarantee success in a notoriously fickle industry (and I personally would not trust any book that purported to do this). But good preparation and training will go a long way to maximising chances of realising ambitions and dreams – or to help someone come to the painful decision that maybe it isn't for them after all.

Acknowledgements

My thanks to everyone who has contributed over the years to my understanding of the craft and the art of acting. Also, grateful thanks to Annie Tyson (Drama Centre), Christian Burgess (Guildhall), Nona Sheppard (RADA), Peter Barlow and Gerry Tebbutt (GSA) and Geoff Colman (Central). Grateful thanks also to Nick Hern and Matt Applewhite for their enthusiasm and support.

Helen Freeman

1

Making the Decision

Why do you want to be an actor? What is acting? What do you have to offer? What are your strengths and weaknesses? What is the profession like?

The decision to train as an actor should come after much researching and soul-searching. Acting is an extremely exacting business and the place to begin is by asking yourself the tough questions above.

Why do you want to be an actor?

Be honest – is this 'Because I want to be famous'? One of the questions most often asked of an actor is 'What have you done that I might have seen you in?' The tart response might be 'Everything I've done, since it had an audience!' However, a more correct translation of the question is 'What *famous* thing have you been in?' and whilst this might be forgivable from someone not in the profession, you probably won't hear it from someone who is. But why not?

Because fame in itself is not acting. It isn't anything but a by-product of what you do. And just as being famous doesn't necessarily mean that you're talented and good at what you do, so not being famous doesn't mean you aren't talented or good at what you do. You do, however, want to be *successful*.

What does 'being successful' mean?

Success in acting means working in a profession that you love, even if that work is not in the forefront of much publicity.

For example, meaningful work might be in Theatre in Education (in schools or institutions, for example). Important work might be in repertory or fringe production, and valid work might be in a profit-share company. Meaningful work might be on stage or on screen (big or small), or on radio. Whatever it is, success means work. But it involves more than just the work you're lucky enough to do.

When you're working

From your first moment as an actor you are going to have other people forming an opinion of you and what you can do, so before you begin, ask yourself: What am I like? What can I offer? What are my strengths and weaknesses? Take an objective look at your talents, skills, physicality and personality. Ask people to critique objectively what you do. (Speaking personally, mothers aren't always the right people to ask!)

Learn how to listen to and work with other people, how to take criticism and how to consider it carefully before accepting or rejecting it. Constructive criticism doesn't mean hearing what you want to hear!

This honesty in self-appraisal will stand you in good stead for a profession that can praise or ridicule in equal measure, often arbitrarily and just as often for exactly the same thing.

Self-appraisal will also build foundations of confidence constructed on more than 'I really want this more than anything/anyone else.' Bear in mind that *everyone* who auditions for a place in drama school believes that they want it more than anyone else and, whilst this desire may help them to focus, it is by no means enough to make anyone give them what they want. Indeed, it begs the response: 'Okay, but why should the profession want you more than anyone else?'

And an honest self-appraisal will show you how you can improve your skills base. These improving skills, your attitude and discipline are the qualities that will help you succeed in a business where the vast majority do not. You are your own brand and yours is the task of shaping and marketing that brand: 'You'.

While we're considering the type of people actors are, it might be a good idea to consider what they're *not*. Actors are not 'normal', in the sense that they wish to earn their living by exploring the condition of mankind and then publicly using what they've learnt for the entertainment/ instruction of others. But neither are they 'abnormal', in that they still have rent or mortgages to pay, food to buy and bills to cover, just like anyone else.

Actors can sometimes be labelled as dizzy 'luvvies' (whatever that means) but don't be fooled. Cultivate the dizzy image if you wish, but develop clear and down-to-earth thinking skills as well. The word on the grapevine is that the average working year for a professional actor is under twelve weeks, which means at least forty weeks 'resting' (the euphemism for being out of acting work). It doesn't make you fail if you think that this might apply to you. On the contrary, you're more likely to work harder to make sure you don't end up as a statistic. Be determined.

When you're not working

So, you work for twelve weeks a year (maybe), but you have to pay bills for fifty-two weeks. Indeed, not only will you have 'ordinary' bills, but you will also have certain extras that many other people don't. For example, photographs of the 8" x 10" variety; showreels containing examples of your work; websites (increasingly vital); subscriptions to various publications and organisations; vocal and movement classes; theatre and cinema visits; travelling to auditions; union and publicity subscriptions, etc., etc. And these expenses continue whether you are in work or not, because the last thing you can do is turn up for an audition looking like you haven't worked, washed or eaten in weeks.

All this is not to depress you, but to get you thinking right now of what you will do to keep the money coming in. You can prepare yourself by having skills up your sleeve before you begin. If you're resting, these other skills should allow you to find a 'normal' job where you can also take time off at the drop of a hat to go for an audition. You need to work during hours that will allow you to keep up with your all-important voice and dance classes (yes, even after you've trained!). You simply have to be creative and think 'outside of the box'.

Some non-acting jobs

- There is always a healthy market for people with good touch-typing and IT skills. The opportunities for temporary work are great and the pay isn't bad, particularly if you have a specialism to offer (for example, medical or legal secretarial skills). One of the bonuses of doing this is that you can vary where you work and you don't need to become involved in 'office politics'.
- A TEFL course (Teaching English as a Foreign Language). This will enable you to obtain qualifications in teaching English to the many business and tourist visitors from abroad.
- If your vocal and/or dance skills are good enough you could take some teaching qualifications (or the preliminaries to these, at least) to obtain work in one of the many children's drama, singing and dancing classes.

- A beauty-therapy course (training as a nail technician or masseur, for example). It goes without saying that you need to be very thorough in your research to make sure that you study only on a bona fide course, but there are evening classes that can offer flexible earning opportunities later.

- Photography classes can also bring surprising benefits. For example, each and every actor needs to have specialist black-and-white photographs taken that are used by schools, agents, casting directors, and on their websites, etc. Perhaps more importantly, every acting student needs them, too, as they leave drama school (and university) each year.

The point is – whatever you do, whatever new skills you learn, use your time now as fruitfully as you can to make life easier later.

So now you've asked yourself the questions about why you want to act and what you understand acting to be about and you've come up with answers more convincing than 'fame' (or plain desire). You've made the decision and you're going to be determined, positive and creative. You are going to be an actor!

Summary

Ask yourself the following questions:
- Why do I want to be an actor?
- What is acting?
- What do I have to offer?
- What are my strengths and weaknesses? What is the profession like?
- How could I use my time now to learn skills that will help me earn while I'm training and afterwards?

Practical

Start to make a list of personal attributes, also asking other people you respect for their opinions:

- VOICE   How do I speak? How quickly do I speak? What does my voice sound like? Do I have a strong accent?
- BODY   How do I stand, sit and walk? Do I shuffle, for example?
- ME   How do I appear to other people? Do I smile and laugh a lot? Am I self-conscious? Do I have mannerisms that other people recognise?

2

University or Drama School?

The value of training

You are determined on a career in acting and you are now in a position to consider your options for training after the age of eighteen. Everyone knows that there are no formal requirements for being an actor but various studies carried out have shown that upwards of eighty per cent of actors in the United Kingdom have received some sort of vocational training.

Caution should be used if you haven't put in the work and you want to pit yourself against someone who has had vocal, movement and theory training. They will also have had the benefit of lectures and workshops on the business itself, which is another advantage.

University versus drama school or conservatoire

If you want to study Drama or Theatre Studies at university, you should be aware that university training does not necessarily have the same primary goal as drama school training. Many students arrive at their drama school auditions having dropped out of university because the theory work was much more intensive, and practical work featured much less than they anticipated.

A matter of hot debate currently, and something you need to check during your research, is the number of 'contact hours' you can expect on your course. This relates to the very practical nature of drama school work and the number of hours per week that you will spend with your tutors working on your skills base. It also refers to the staffing and delivery of the course. The discrepancy between the number and experience of tutors and the number of hours they will spend with you each week can be marked when drama school and university courses are compared. It can also sometimes be telling to ask yourself, 'How many hours am I being *trained* here?', since the acting process often requires a more holistic process that is inextricably linked to practical discipline.

The courses do vary in practical content from institution to institution but primarily, do not expect or simply accept that a university will actively make you an actor and fit for today's profession. It is perfectly reasonable to make such enquiries as part of your research.

This does not mean that you cannot pursue drama school training on completion of your university degree – many people do and the benefits are tremendous, both to themselves and to others on the acting course. However, it will have funding implications (beware of the continually moving goalposts here), so check carefully with your local authority. For example, funding for a second degree in the arts is not currently in place.

Making the decision

You owe it to yourself (and to the person whose place at university you might take) to do your research and make absolutely certain that the practical/vocational content of the course is what you are looking for as a springboard to your chosen career.

The course title doesn't always help. 'Theatre Studies', for example, can mean a course structured around theory at one university but much more practical work at another. The use of 'Acting' in the title can help marginally, but the only way to ensure that the course content is what you are looking for is to obtain prospectuses, attend open days, showcases and productions, and do your research well before you need to make up your mind.

Think of why you would opt for university training instead of drama school training. This is hugely personal and many factors can apply in the decision-making process.

For example, students who want to be playwrights, directors or producers sometimes don't want to go to drama school because they want a broader and more inclusive study of theory that feeds their artistic ideas (although there are also some very good directing and writing courses at drama school). Or they may not yet know which branch of the profession they wish to go into and may not want to commit to any one school's own particular ethos.

Alternatively, you may feel that to study an additional subject with drama increases your options post-training, or you may want to attend with a variety of people studying on completely different courses.

Moreover, whilst drama schools offer more degree and diploma variation than they used to, traditional university drama degrees can still be regarded in a more positive light in the wider workplace (rightly or wrongly), even though the profession of acting might well give no weight to them.

The upshot is that you do need to ask some hard questions of any degree course whether at drama school or university. For example, how will you want a degree to work for you afterwards? No actor needs a degree to act, but make sure you know what credit is given by other professions to a degree in acting from a drama school as opposed to a university. Make sure you know about the alternative post-training options and statistics from any specific drama school.

A possible pitfall

The waters have been muddied by the route of application for some of the drama schools and conservatoires. UCAS (Universities and Colleges Admissions Service) is the body that governs the university-admissions procedure and some drama schools have begun to audition only those who apply through UCAS. Moreover, there is also a specialised online admissions service which processes applications to some dance and drama programmes at UK conservatoires.

This is not something to be overwhelmingly concerned about so long as the school confirms that *everyone* applying is offered an audition, given that talent and aptitude are and have always been the criteria for an actor. Also, check to see if there's an accompanying proviso stating that talent will outweigh the exam results expected, given that talent is unrelated to academic ability and/or results. If the prospectus doesn't specifically say so – ask them!

Some drama schools have not guaranteed any such audition, basing their decision on your personal statement on the UCAS form. In my opinion, a personal statement like this gives very little indication of what you are like emotionally or intellectually as an actor, and no information at all on how talented you are. Moreover, your personal statement may have been written for multiple applications to both university drama courses and drama school courses – each of which demands its own approach – and yours may turn out to be an unsatisfactory hybrid if you don't take great care.

In any event, talk to your teachers and tutors to decide how best to avoid the quandary of a personal statement that is not appropriate to university, conservatoire or drama school, and which might well result in failure where an audition/interview is not automatic.

Studying unrelated subjects at university

Each situation and each individual is different, but suffice it to say that if you are determined to be an actor, then it is perfectly possible to do so via any route in life. Acting is about life, after all, so all of your experience adds to your potential, and there are a fair few of today's actors who have gone into the business from another profession. That said, you need to be very determined with your extra-curricular preparation and have a serious look at all your options, from a postgraduate or short course to another full-time drama school course (bearing in mind all funding implications at the point of application). Trying to make your way in the acting profession when you have not trained is not easy (nor is it easy when you have) so care should be taken if this is how you want to proceed. After all, drama students do not spend three years doing nothing!

Training in technique is a prerequisite of any good drama school course along with sometimes quite arduous physical work to ensure fitness for purpose. You need to make certain that your university course will comply with this – even if it is a course run by a drama school that has become part of a university (such as Drama Centre, East 15 or GSA, for example).

Starting to prepare

The next chapter will begin to look more specifically at the areas you need to consider in your preparation, but for now you need to remember that a large part of performance for the future professional is 'educational'. In other words, stay loose and flexible, so you can learn and evolve as an artist in the art form.

Whether you are dancing or singing, working on your under-standing, or feeding your curiosity of life by sitting in a library or café watching people – 'development' is your key word.

Simply picking up the bag and baggage of a 'style' of performance will not give your performance content and quality. Always examine what you are learning through objective eyes and include your whole life in this process, to help you avoid any possible bad habits like clichéd 'acting' and instant characterisation.

These can be big let-downs at auditions for drama school because they show inflexibility in a creative art form that should remain fluid and organic. Your unique personality can be hidden from view, which is disastrous (see one of the BBC Shakespeare DVDs, for example, to observe how many of these wonderful actors do their job. Watch and analyse – but don't copy). You must begin to see yourself as a creative person who should be as organically rooted in the truth as the art form itself.

The demands of drama school

Whatever your choice of drama school, an acting student will have many demands placed on them that may well come as a shock if they are not prepared. Maturity and discipline are but two of these demands, and by carefully making your choices you are already on your way to achieving these at least.

Entrance

Entry to drama school is extremely competitive! Thousands of students apply each year and the acceptance on to an acting course can be as low as one per cent, with fewer than one thousand acting and musical-theatre students graduating each year from drama school.

Whilst no drama school is going to limit itself come what may, the number of females admitted as drama students can sometimes be fewer than males (although at the time of writing, RADA, for example, accept twenty-eight students onto the BA (Hons) in Acting each year, in the ratio of fourteen men and fourteen women, whatever the number of applicants).

Unfortunately, however cross we might feel about it, an unequal admission proportion only reflects a business in which there is generally more work for males yet female application is higher. Drama schools will continually try to find the best and fairest way to treat art form, business and student, so perhaps this is another question to ask them about when you're considering where to apply.

Again, all this is not to dishearten, but to give you a more specific idea of the difficulties (and realities) of the profession, which is no bad thing. Forewarned is forearmed, so don't be depressed!

Age restrictions

Applicants for full-time courses must be eighteen (twenty-one for postgraduate courses), but should you need to pay your way through training there are also many part-time courses at drama schools that are structured to fit in as much as possible with normal working lives. This could mean working on your skills base during your gap year, for example, which would help you if and when you come to audition for the full three-year course.

At this juncture, I should point out that no drama school or conservatoire worth its salt should look disparagingly at someone who has taken time out after school to see life, leave home, travel, work and generally grow up before they apply. Indeed, a good spread of ages in any undergraduate acting programme is popular, so while some people may be ready in experience and talent at eighteen, many (the majority) need some extra time and life experience. There is no shame and absolutely no real disadvantage to this.

The drama school routine

Quite apart from the emotional work that goes on, the working day at a drama school involves much physical work, so your level of fitness must be high. Acting is not for people who shy away from committed movement, and every acting course will have many types of dance and movement as an important part of it. Physical stamina and staying power are two very important attributes that will only stand you in good stead for the future.

So in your pre-training time find a fitness regime that suits you. If you intend to pursue a career in musical theatre then you should be adding regular dance classes to that regime; ballet at the very least, for the many benefits of line and posture.

Both actors and musical-theatre students can also expect a varying mix of classes in singing and vocal technique as well as theatre history and acting theory (which will differ from school to school).

Choosing which drama school

As already mentioned, each drama school varies in the ethos, approach and content of their course (not to mention type of institution!), so it is important to thoroughly investigate each school and course to ensure that it accords with your personal needs and goals.

However, whilst you may well feel certain that you want to train for one particular branch of performance at the moment (musical theatre as opposed to 'straight' acting, for example), I would not advise making too many decisions about more detailed career choices (such as screen work instead of theatre work) before you have embarked on a training course. You will develop and change quite 'dramatically' over your three years of training, so keep an open and fertile mind. One ex-student of mine is now absorbed in classical acting, having previously been set on a career in musical theatre. For now, focus simply on being the very best that you can be.

That said, if you *are* considering a musical-theatre option, you will have to pay more attention to the course breakdown, since the proportions of training spent on each of the three disciplines of acting, singing and dancing (all three of which make up the 'triple-threat performer') can vary a good deal (and this is looked at in more detail later).

Other expectations of you

Acting is a tremendously disciplined art form – so whatever your personal habits, you will also be expected:

- To be punctual for all your classes and rehearsals (some schools now operate the system of 'locking' the door to latecomers at the time the class is due to commence). Lack of punctuality in the profession leads to lack of employment – word does get around!
- To be enthusiastic, energised and 'hungry'.

Public performance

Even if you get the chance to perform publicly quite soon into your course, this 'performance' may take the form of a rehearsed reading in front of your fellow students and the teaching staff. The school will decide how it wants to build in performance opportunities until you are developed and skilled enough to be seen by agents and the general public in your important final productions.

In addition, some schools allow a certain amount of time during training when you can be 'released' to work. Others don't; it's all a matter of an individual school's ethos. There are good reasons both for and against this (not least of all the training basis of the school). It goes without saying that you should be cautious about wanting to perform too quickly. If you make the right decision in terms of the school at which you train, you can also trust their advice on this point.

The necessity of preparation

Two things here. Firstly, remember the statistics about your competition for a place. You need to be ready for the big day of your audition if you want to stand out in the right way.

Secondly, while it is fair to say that at each drama school you will study varying amounts of stagecraft and professionalism (the business of being an actor, the thrust of this depending, as ever, on the individual school's philosophy), it is not fair to assume that any school will be able to teach you every element of being an actor from scratch to consummate professional in just three years.

The course will speed by and (in most cases at least) there simply isn't enough time for you to learn the basics and then take them to the standard required for you to apply your knowledge practically and professionally. This is why you should put yourself at an advantage with a good amount of preparation before you apply, so you will be in a good position to gain a place and then to begin your first year, which lays the foundations of the skills you'll build upon.

Summary

- Where do I see myself in five years' time? How do I want my qualifications and training to work for me?

Practical

- Start to investigate university and/or drama school courses, in their prospectuses or online.

- Perfect your own personal statement for your application forms in line with the courses that interest you. Ask for advice from everyone in the know, but remember at least to:

  ‣ Make it clear that you understand the balance of the course.

  ‣ Support your fitness for this course and this balance.

  ‣ Give an indication of any experience and particular interests you have (for example, your favourite playwright/type of theatre/ productions you have seen and enjoyed).

❝ Choose wisely – think about the courses and look at the department. Do not be put off by what anybody else thinks, it's not just about what you're good at, it's about what you enjoy. Drama is a widely respected method of third-level training and it opens many doors into many careers. This is particularly the case with a degree. It's almost a training for life.

Chris (BA Drama and Theatre Arts, Trinity College Dublin)

3

The Key to Preparation

You've decided on becoming an actor and you've also decided on going to drama school as opposed to university. Now is the time to prepare for your audition and to begin to form the good habits that will help you in your career.

This chapter looks at the preparation and opportunities that begin in secondary school, and at some of the practical things you can do to maximise your development potential.

It's very depressing that that many of our young hopefuls simply do not *do* enough: to sharpen their all-important curiosity, to feed their knowledge and to develop their understanding of the art form to which they wish to devote themselves – even though these are the qualities that will make them such a tempting proposition to the powers that be. Don't let yourself be one of them!

If it all goes wrong

It's important to reassure yourself and your parents, who might feel concerned that this kind of commitment will jeopardise your potential in any other area. Rest assured that your personal development, social and life skills (not to mention self-discipline) will come in very useful down the line – whatever career you eventually embark upon.

It's also important to understand that you are unique, and this uniqueness will help you in the profession.

Specialist stage schools

It is not necessary for you to leave your 'normal' school and attend a specialist school, no matter how talented or serious you are about becoming an actor. Granted, you might have to hunt around for extra-curricular dancing and singing classes in your area, but attending a stage school or specialist performing arts school is no more of a guarantee of success. Nor will it prepare you according to your own needs. And nor is it specifically endorsed by the industry experts as being an ideal way into the profession. It can also close down options and life experience which may be invaluable to an actor.

GCSE Drama

Drama has grown into a very popular school subject in recent years – and with good reason given the benefits of studying the subject, not only to those interested in the profession but to all students. GCSE Drama is not a prerequisite for your future success, but it can start the ball rolling as far as certain skills are concerned. You will be introduced to the ideas of expressing yourself and communicating a playwright's intentions, for example. You will also begin to explore improvisation, and learn to respond both emotionally and intellectually to drama.

Use this work to help you become observant, both of other people and of yourself. Your confidence and powers of concentration will then grow.

Courses for sixteen- to eighteen-year-olds

There are various courses that your school might offer after GCSEs. Some are more practical than others, but they are all interesting and should sharpen your curiosity of life and people, as well as performance. You will probably not be able to choose which specific exam-board syllabus you take since your school will decide which is most appropriate for them to teach. Rest assured that none is better than the others in the long-term scheme of things.

- A-Level Drama and Theatre Studies (and the English Irish Leaving Certificate drama component) can involve more theoretical work than practical work and are often studied prior to university entrance, but many people do also go on to drama school after these courses. Your developing skills will benefit from the live theatre requirements as well as from the components designed to encourage you to think independently and to work imaginatively and sensitively in a group, listening to others' ideas.

- BTEC courses in the performing arts are more practical in nature and offer optional units in singing and music, stagecraft, drama, dance and movement (among others).

- Highers and Higher National Certificates and Diplomas are the Scottish alternatives to the above, including choices in Dance, Acting and Performance and Musical Theatre (as well as others).

Do remember, though, that an A-Level, BTEC or Higher is *not* professional acting training. Neither are they prerequisites to being a professional actor and many wonderful actors never took any of them!

We're talking about using these courses as opportunities for you to learn about yourself and how to listen to and work with others, as well as learning about theatre terminology and practice through the texts and practitioners you'll study and the live theatre you'll see and perform. But trust your drama school to give you the tools you'll need professionally. It's what they're there for – and what they're renowned the world over for.

School productions

You will undoubtedly have the opportunity to appear in a number of school productions. Enjoy these. They're wonderful confidence-building projects and you can learn a great deal about yourself and your skills from participating in them.

National Youth Theatre and National Youth Music Theatre

Performance experience will also help your ongoing preparation and development of your personal attributes. A very good opportunity to gain experience comes with the National Youth Theatre (NYT) and National Youth Music Theatre (NYMT). Look on the websites of these companies who hold courses at various times (including during the summer) which build towards exciting performances at the end of them (see Appendix for website addresses).

These organisations provide very useful introductions to working on specific performance projects with a larger number of other young people, many of whom will go on to audition at drama school.

If you apply for the NYT or the NYMT you are guaranteed an audition and it is useful to experience the competitive edge of your chosen profession in such a supported structure. At the time of writing, over four thousand applications are received by them annually for about six hundred residential-course places (plus a further one hundred and fifty regional-course places). You can also join a weekly drama class and may have the opportunity to participate in a community programme.

If you are lucky enough to be offered a place, your self-discipline will develop, along with your self-esteem and confidence, and you'll gain valuable insights into connecting with your work (an essential thing, as you'll see later). Your group skills will be emphasised from the audition on, since the morning session of the audition itself can comprise a workshop.

You can either apply online, choosing the best venue for your audition and paying the fee by credit or debit card (with all necessary permissions, it goes without saying), or you can download and complete the application form from their websites.

For your audition you'll need to prepare a two-minute speech from any play (not a film or TV script). This is also one – possibly the only – case where they do not mind if you take the speech from a school production, but wherever it comes from, you do need to know the full play and have some ideas about it.

Amateur dramatics societies

Of course, one of the most popular ways of gaining performance experience is as the member of an amateur dramatics society. If you are tempted to do this, then you can look online for a company in your area. Or you can visit the website of the Little Theatre Guild (see Appendix), an association of amateur theatre companies who own or control their theatre buildings, to check whether there is a member company local to you.

The advantage of joining a society which is a member of the Little Theatre Guild is that their aims include the promotion and development of young people's involvement in theatre and youth theatre groups. They also have a policy of monitoring the standards of all their members.

For example, if you live in London, you may have the opportunity to join The Questors in Ealing. This company has a reputation for achieving very high standards in the twenty or so shows they mount each year in their theatre complex. They offer the chance to audition every month, but if you have very little acting experience then you might be able to audition for the Questors Acting Foundation course. This is a one-year, part-time course which will build your confidence and commitment through speech and movement classes at weekends and in the evenings (see Appendix).

As you enjoy and learn as much as you can from your work with any amateur company, remember to keep looking objectively at what you're doing. Compare it with the work you want to be doing in the profession and with the work of the students graduating from the drama schools.

Whatever you do and wherever you choose to gain your experience, be careful not to develop bad habits of clichéd performance style or inflexibility. All these will do is disconnect you from the truth of what you're trying to do, which is the essential quality that the drama schools will be looking for.

Youth theatre groups

Many theatre companies all over Britain give homes to youth theatre groups, which can be brilliant for gaining valuable experience. For example, TAG Theatre Company in Glasgow is attached to the Citizens Theatre and has been providing tremendous theatre and educational activities for young people since 1967. Equally, at the Royal Exchange Theatre in Manchester there are several youth theatre groups – the First Bite Theatre Group in the eleven-to-fourteen age bracket, to the Young People's Theatre Workshop for fourteen- to nineteen-year-olds. Alternatively, if you live near London, you could join the Old Vic New Voices scheme. They have Creative Learning projects where eight- to twenty-five-year-olds can learn on the famous Old Vic stage and attend many wonderful masterclasses and workshops. You can also purchase tickets for the Old Vic shows at reduced prices. And there's the Theatre Royal Haymarket's Masterclass scheme, offering free talks and workshops to anyone aged between seventeen and thirty. The list of Masterclass leaders is like a Who's Who of British theatre, including Steven Berkoff, Derek Jacobi, Ruthie Henshall, Nicholas Hytner, Joanna Lumley, Helen Mirren and many more (see Appendix for details of all these groups).

Theatre and cinema visits

Ironically, one of the most often ignored pieces of advice is to go to the theatre to see as much as possible. By 'theatre' I mean *plays* as well as musicals, and physical theatre performances as well as dance.

Don't make the mistake of thinking that you don't need to see plays if you are only interested (at the moment) in musical theatre. Many good musicals are taken from an original source that almost certainly wasn't musical in form: *My Fair Lady* is based on George Bernard Shaw's *Pygmalion*; *West Side Story* is a retelling of *Romeo and Juliet*; *Les Misérables*, *Oliver!* and *Wicked* are all based on novels. The rich complexities of character need to be studied in isolation to the song and dance if you want your technique to be informed by it. Certainly, you should not be attending multiple performances of the same musical if it is at the expense of seeing some productions of plays as well.

Theatre tickets can be dreadfully expensive, but you have an absolute obligation to broaden your theatrical experience and deepen your theatrical knowledge (you also need to know where your profession is and where it's going). There are often discounts available for students at individual theatres (check the annual 'Get Into London Theatre' season, for example), and there are many other theatres and smaller companies throughout the UK that offer the opportunity to see good work at less exorbitant prices, so scout around. NT Live broadcasts major productions from the National Theatre and other theatres to cinemas around the UK and internationally, so it's an excellent opportunity to see high-quality work on the big screen, at cheaper prices, and closer to home.

Studying on an A-Level, BTEC or Highers course will give you many opportunities to see, discuss and analyse performances with your teacher. But you must also go to professional performances to start developing your own critical eye. Analysing a production for a written exam is something quite different from the professional eye that you need, and your teacher may or may not have professional performance experience.

At the risk of adding more to your preparation, try to read the texts of the plays that resonate with you when you've seen a production. If you connect with any role in a particular play, read the whole play thoroughly. Reading plays should become one of your hobbies (and ideally you should try to read them before you go to see them in production!).

Singing lessons

While you are still at school is the time to take some singing lessons, at least sufficient to give you a practice CD to follow between lessons.

Singing lessons may form part of an A-Level or other exam, but even if they don't it is not possible to stress enough how useful singing lessons can be in helping you to form the good breathing habits that help all actors. It goes without saying that it matters even more if you intend to become a musical-theatre performer. But all actors need to be able to support the voice with the breath and to develop a system that will translate to a strong, good technique.

Again, finance may be an issue but if you can afford even some lessons you can rest in the knowledge that you are already working towards maximising your chances of acceptance at drama school. You may find that your music teacher at school has some recommendations of singing tutors – or may even be able to teach you themselves. Personal recommendation is the best way to find a good teacher. One of the reasons for this is that there is no governing body of singing teachers, as such, so as a professional colleague once said: 'If you don't hear and feel improvement – stop and find yourself another teacher!' You could begin by looking at the websites for the Association of Singing and Music Teachers (see Appendix) for some advice.

Dancing lessons

I would also strongly advise all potential musical-theatre students to find some way of incorporating dance training into their weekly schedule, and as far in advance of your drama school application as possible. Not much may be on offer where you live, but do your best to attend a regular ballet and/or tap/jazz class at the very least. Many students competing for the few places will demonstrate good technique and expertise, and it is doubtful whether you will make it through to a place on one of the hotly contested courses without being able to convince the audition panel of your potential and determination.

You should also be keeping yourself at a good level of fitness, playing sport or going to the gym (obviously supervised and conducted with care). Any of these will help your core muscle strength, coordination, fitness and stamina levels (even if they don't do much in themselves to develop dance technique, posture or your 'line').

There is advice on different types of dance and where you can learn on the International Dance Teachers Association (IDTA) website (see Appendix).

Acting lessons

Individual acting classes working towards a LAMDA, Trinity and Guildhall or VCM (Victoria College of Music) examination can all be taken while you're at school. RADA Shakespeare Certificate exams can also be studied and the work you will do with your teacher on any of these courses should begin to address some of the issues you'll need to consider later in voice production and contextual knowledge, for example.

These classes are normally held on a weekly basis leading up to exams either at a public or private centre (in the case of RADA or LAMDA, for instance, they can also be taken at their own premises, which gives you a chance to get a feel of the school).

Acting coaching

There are many advertisements for acting coaching, particularly for 'audition technique' and these words of advice from someone in the profession can sometimes prove invaluable, especially if that professional knows you personally.

But (could you hear the 'but' coming?) these one-to-one sessions can be expensive, will not help you with the ensemble nature of acting and are not at all guaranteed to be either useful or valid for you in your drama school audition, unless the coach is experienced in teaching and working in drama schools. Moreover, you risk your pieces becoming so polished and 'directed' that the raw talent the panel will be looking for can be subsumed. Remember, a good performer with stunning credits does not necessarily make a good teacher.

Intensive personal coaching is not a necessity for success in the audition room (and it might prove to be an expensive hindrance), but if you are determined that finding a coach is the thing for you, then the most sensible thing you could do is ring a drama school and ask for their advice and recommendations. They may be either unwilling or unable to help you (because of conflict of interest or staffing issues), but nothing ventured, nothing gained.

School holidays and weekend courses

Outside your school term-time there are holiday courses in acting and musical theatre, often at the drama schools you will be considering later.

This can be a good way to judge the feel of a drama school prior to attending an audition, or to see the facilities they have and the approach they favour.

Do remember, however, that no good drama school is going to commit themselves to taking you on their full-time three-year course without your having reached the requisite standards for that course, whether you have attended a weekend or holiday school with them or not. But these courses can be hugely helpful and, if you can afford them, will give you many benefits for the future.

Remember, too, that you are seeing if they meet *your* requirements as well, which leads us to the next stage in your preparation: researching the drama schools themselves.

Summary

- What am I doing right now to prepare for going to drama school? What can I do to make the best use of my time and money in acting/singing/dancing?
- What playtexts have I read recently? What character in any play have I seen that I connected with? Was that to do with the actor who played that role? If so, where did s/he train?
- What productions and films have I seen?

Practical

- Decide which production you are going to see next and make a point of reading the text before you go.
- If you are a potential musical-theatre performer, make a list of musicals and their original source material to see how many good ones come from non-musical forms (additions to your reading list!).
- Find out what extra-curricular activities you might be able to attend.

66 What I really obtained from university was that it allowed me to grow up and mature in a place in which I was surrounded by an eclectic bunch of people. Without this, I don't think I could have coped with drama school. I am glad that I went to university, met lots of different people, took a gap year, worked in a butcher's shop and on a building site. Then on my postgrad course I had an amazing year and learned so much. I think that drama school suits some people at eighteen and university suits others. For me, university gave me three years' more maturity and a broader mind.

Harry (BA Drama & Theatre Arts, Birmingham University;
MA Postgraduate Acting for Screen, Central School
of Speech and Drama)

4

Research, Research, Research

So, you've got the prospectuses of all the schools you've heard about plus maybe one or two that your research has thrown up. The important thing to realise at this stage is that while all the major drama schools share many ideas, viewpoints and goals, they are different in their approach to the training of their students.

Some of them have an approach linked to a particular theory of acting whilst others take elements of many different theories. Others still may seem more readily to turn out screen actors instead of stage actors, or musical-theatre performers rather than 'straight' actors.

It is important to do your homework to help you draw up a shortlist of schools that meet your list of priorities. How comfortable do you feel when you're looking round them, for example? This feeling can be very strong, and as I've said before, you are actively choosing your school just as they will actively choose you. Looking around your shortlisted schools might help you to avoid making some fundamental mistake that could see you dropping out later.

Where to begin

Definitely not the be-all and end-all of choosing, but a good place to begin is by looking at the alumni of a school. All of the drama schools are rightly very proud of their students as representatives of what the school is striving for (see Appendix for examples).

You will obtain a good idea of the type of performer produced at a school from considering their alumni's work. Also, many of these actors have commented on their training and their comments are worth reading. Do bear in mind, however, any radical changes that might have taken place in the time since they graduated. A wonderful actor of forty years ago, for example, might find today's profession much harder to live with and the school they attended may have changed the training ethos substantially, to keep up with the changing profession. But the work of the school's graduates is as good a place as any to start.

When you go to see a production, read the programme notes on the actors before it begins, so you can familiarise yourself with their training, their work and technique.

And remember the personal-experience books that will help you, too. For example, *Being An Actor* by Simon Callow (Penguin) or *Other People's Shoes* by Harriet Walter (Nick Hern Books).

Reading the prospectuses

You're forming an opinion of a school's ethos from reading what it presents about itself. For example, when did the school start, by whom, and what was their driving reason? Don't be fooled by a glossy prospectus and/or a glitzy website. Look, rather, for all the nuggets of information on how your training will be shaped by their ruling principles. For instance, how are they dealing with the huge changes that are taking place in our modern-day art form?

All of this is helping to shape your ideas of what you want and how you might get it.

Taking a closer look

Now you need to get a feel for those schools on your short-list, so take the opportunity to do this before your formal audition. You are a prospective house buyer, if you like. Your goal is that after three years of training, you will leave drama school proficient and confident, an actor at home in him/herself, a force to be reckoned with.

When all's said and done it's how *you* instinctively respond to a school that will make the difference to what you put in and take out of a course. Don't be embarrassed about being up front with this – whilst all drama schools will deliver the very best training they can, remember that acting, not being an exact science, has many strands on which to concentrate and these will vary from school to school.

As we've seen, the number of students admitted each year may range from fifteen to thirty-four (give or take). Much will depend on the way the school works and, given the feel of a particular school, you may consider that fewer students might give you more of the one-to-one time that's needed. On the other hand, you might be wary of the possible draw-backs of a small group (which might or might not be exacerbated by the gender breakdown).

Visit the websites and find out about any open days and/or tours your shortlisted drama schools run. As mentioned before, if you are taking individual classes in acting, you may well have the chance to take the exams for these in the actual facilities of, for example, LAMDA or RADA.

Another very useful way in which you can learn about a school is by seeing their graduates in action as they are about to enter the profession.

Each year a school's current crop of third-year actors will perform in their final productions for the public. These are the showcases to which theatrical agents (who represent professional actors) are invited, so you'll get a good idea of the thrust of the school's training, and you may also get an idea of the 'type' of person accepted at that school.

This may sound strange, but the range of schools varies enormously, as will their production approach. Again, try not to judge the costume, set, props and production values of a showcase – you're there to have a searching look at the *actors* the school is turning out, which does not correspond to money spent on a production.

It can sometimes be illuminating to check the casting in more than one showcase or final production. A student actor's CV will show the range of roles undertaken during their training. What you are looking for is the experience they have been given of playing both larger and smaller parts, as well as the type of parts they have been cast in. It is important that a young actor is trained to shine as a minor character and to carry a show as a lead, for example, to maximise their employability when they leave.

Fine-tune your shortlist of schools

You've got a list of the schools that interest you. Note the word 'list' here, because although it can be counterproductive to audition for every drama school in the country, you do need to audition for several schools to get a good idea of what drama schools are and what you're looking for, as well as to familiarise yourself with the audition process.

Ask more questions

To help with the process of elimination, it's back to the prospectus and website to find out a few more things.

- Look at the list of directors and teaching staff to see what links the school has with the profession. How 'cutting edge' are they with the needs of a changing profession? Where did their teachers train? Also, do they still work in the profession and, if so, who might teach you in their absence to ensure continuity and quality in your training?

- How much studio, rehearsal and performance space (or external provision) is there? What plans are there for any expansion?

- Does the school have plans to amalgamate with any other school and/or to move premises? If so, then you have some more research to do to find out which other school is joining them and to see if the approaches are sympathetic. For example, what changes will actually be made to the facilities, the timetable or the approach the school will take?

- What is the timetable breakdown? This will give you a good idea of how the training is shaped. What proportions of time are spent on voice work or movement, theory or practice, for example? These will all inform you of the approach of the school and the practical side of what they offer – and may well raise more questions to ask.

- What's the proportion of teaching for screen as opposed to stage (and the facilities for this)? Although you will not want to limit yourself by decisions yet, you do need to ensure that your training covers all aspects of an actor's workplace.

Remember that just as theatres and theatre companies, like the Royal Court, Stratford East, the Traverse, the National Theatre or Punchdrunk, all produce different fare, so do drama schools.

Once you've thoroughly researched your options and have reached this stage you'll have a much clearer idea of what's going on in the profession, in the schools and in yourself. It's a process for developing your curiosity and your independence of thought; you should be building your knowledge and focusing your ambition.

Summary

- Use the prospectus and the website of each school, as well as any newspaper articles or production reviews, to inform your process of shortlisting drama schools.

- Use your individual acting or singing exams (if they're held on the school premises) to reconnoitre the school.

- Use current professional productions and programmes to look at the actors the school has turned out and see what interviews/comments there may be.

- Research what a school has to offer in the way of teaching staff/links with the profession, facilities and course content.

Practical

- Find out when the third-year students are performing in their showcases, and go and see them (there are usually discounts available so get used to asking for them).

- While you're at the show, see if there are any copies available of each student's curriculum vitae which will give you a good idea of the work they have turned out during their training and whether they've already been signed by an agent. A photograph may also be included so you can see what you should be thinking about when considering your own headshots in the future. See how many of them actually have pink hair or multiple body piercings, for example!

Making your application

It goes without saying that you must ensure that you get all the practical details right when applying to drama school. Here are some things to consider about making your application:

- *Timing*

  Many of the schools advise early application – sometimes as soon as you can after mid-September or the beginning of October. This is to ensure an audition date before the deluge of applications. The application cut-off date for many of them is mid-January through to February, although this can vary in flexibility.

- *Cost*

  The cost of auditioning is not cheap, varying approximately from £35 to £50. This will include the preliminary audition and any recalls you may be invited to attend. Be aware that you may also need to factor in accommodation and travelling costs, which will increase the overall expenditure. Be prepared for an overnight stay even if, in theory, you can catch the last train home. Some schools will waive the application fee for students from lower-income families; check websites for details.

- *Extras*

  - Most of the schools ask you to attach a photograph to your application form. This will usually need to be passport-sized, but a full-sized photograph may be required.

  - You must check to see if the school requires references from you and whether these should be academic, professional and/or personal.

  - Most schools will also require you to include a personal statement. In the case of UCAS applications, this is where you must be very careful, since your statement may well have been constructed with universities in mind as well as drama schools, which can confuse matters somewhat. And, as discussed in Chapter Two, there is currently at least one drama school that bases their decision on whether to offer a first-round audition wholly on the applicant's UCAS personal statement.

Always check, check and triple check that you have included all the right documentation and are applying in good time for your schools. Keep referring to the school's application guidelines, as it can be easy to muddle requirements if you are applying to several schools in the same audition season.

Your audition

Each school's prospectus and/or website will give you a lot of information on what they will be looking for at your preliminary audition, and there will also be details in the letter confirming your audition date. You must constantly refer to these details to check that you are doing what you are supposed to be doing!

For example, if it says clearly on the website and in the pack you are sent that three pieces must be prepared (or are advised), then it's going to be a disappointment for all concerned for you to turn up not having prepared a third piece. In effect, you will have limited your own chances to show what you can do.

Equally, do not think that they will not notice if you turn up with the same speech that you've prepared for another school (one that happens to prescribe the speeches they want you to choose from, for example). This often flies in the face of what's appropriate for any other audition and isn't very complimentary, as it shows you haven't done the dedicated work in preparing for this school.

The audition panel

Your preliminary audition will be for a panel of (usually) two people, almost never fewer.

One or both of these will be actual directors or teachers at the school, one may come directly from the profession (director, actor, musical director, for instance).

The form of the audition

All the audition panels will do their best to help you to give *your* best. Rest assured, whatever they ask of you is because they want you to be the one they want. Remember this so you don't panic.

There is a certain amount of variation on a theme in the shape of the very first audition, so check your audition pack and/or the website for details. The best thing is to be prepared to go with the flow of whatever you're asked to do:

- There may be a short chat before you perform your pieces. This is not a formal interview but more to put you at your ease.
- You will perform your pieces.
- You may then be asked to work more intensively on one of them with a panellist (or a current student). For example, to repeat one of your pieces in a different way, perhaps sitting across the table from the panel and quietly speaking to them.
- For a musical-theatre course you will perform your song.
- You might have to sing it again (or part of it) in a slightly different way.
- Alternatively, you may be asked to sing some or all of your 'alternative' song.
- For some of the acting courses, the prepared song will come here (sometimes with an accompanist, sometimes not).

- You may then have to deconstruct that song (saying it as a speech to the panel, for example).
- Some schools' panels may have an informal chat with you now.

The vital thing to remember here is that you must listen, listen, *listen* to what is being said to you. As I said before, all the panel wants is for you to do your very best, and they are experienced enough to know how scary the whole process is for you.

After the audition

Following the preliminary audition, you might either have to wait for a letter to see if you have been successful in gaining a recall or, as is the case with at least one school, you may be able to telephone the day afterwards for the result. Ask whoever is running the administrative side of the audition if the information is not obvious.

More intensive preliminary auditions

On some occasions there may be a wait for an hour or so following your preliminary audition, to see if your name goes up on a list for further first auditioning later that day.

If this is the case, you may have to perform your speeches again – perhaps in a slightly different format or working with the course director, for example. Sometimes this is the stage at which an actor has to sing their song.

There might now be another wait for a final preliminary audition list to go up to see if you've been recalled for an improvisation workshop in the evening, for example.

What next?

However simple or intensive these preliminary auditions have been and whether they have taken place over fifteen minutes or the whole day, the panel will then use their judgement of how you fulfilled the grading criteria of the school, to help them make their decision to invite you to the recall auditions proper. If so, you will then have up to a full weekend of recall auditioning and possibly even a third recall, all of which happen at a later date.

Use the prospectus and website (or your preliminary confirmation letter) to familiarise yourself thoroughly with the detail of each school's audition policy, so you don't feel all at sea on the day. Do not panic, just go with the flow! This is where your preparation can really kick in to support and calm you.

Your pieces

What you are asked to prepare will include any or all of the following. It's wise to have several offerings in each category (definitely more than the school asks for) from which to choose when the formal application is made:

- One, two or three classical speeches (make sure you prepare a sufficient number of the correct speeches). Sometimes these must be a verse speech from Shakespeare (one may even have to be chosen from a list of specific speeches designated by the school). Alternatively, you might be able to choose any Elizabethan or Jacobean piece. Schools will specify the type and length that this is allowed to be, usually no more than two or three minutes, *absolute maximum.* Sometimes only a specified number of lines may be required. Do keep referring to the audition requirements to check, as it can become confusing if you are auditioning for several schools all within a couple of weeks. Mistakes on the day can throw you, as well as annoy the audition panel.

- One or more 'modern', contrasting speeches. The school may specify precisely how modern this must be (for example, post-1960, post-1830, contemporary, etc.). They may even specify the nature of the pieces so make sure you have a good choice for them. Again, the usual length of these is either two or three minutes maximum.

- A song, either accompanied or unaccompanied. (Please see the separate section on specific auditions for musical-theatre courses.) In the event that there is an accompanist you must ensure that you take along a clean copy of the music which:

  ‣ Is in the right key for you (do not expect the accompanist to transpose for you!).

  ‣ Has any cuts clearly marked on it.

  ‣ Has the pages sellotaped together so that they can open out in one long (but not *too* long!) sheet on the piano.

  ‣ Does not exceed the two or three minutes specified.

Follow the instructions

- Prepare exactly what you are asked to prepare, with regards to numbers and types of pieces.
- Do not exceed the time limits on the pieces or the panel may well stop you in mid-flow.

If you 'don't sing'

Please do not be concerned if you are auditioning for an acting course, yet you are being asked to prepare an audition song. This is perfectly normal and no panel is going to judge your singing ability as such. What they are interested in is your ability to *tell the story* of the song, to put it across to an audience.

This does not mean, of course, that you can feel free to murder a song by not rehearsing it, for you must be able to carry the tune to the best of your ability and act it confidently (read Chapter Seven on musical-theatre auditions for hints on preparation).

Ideally, by the time you are applying to drama schools, you will have a choice of speeches (and songs for musical-theatre applicants), and will have enough knowledge of the schools to be able to choose which is the right combination to perform for each audition.

Remember your aim is to show, through your work, who you are as a person and as a performer.

66 Keep sight of the individual. Be selfish – but compassionate – and relish every moment. Don't lose confidence in yourself and if you enjoy a certain aspect of your training, explore it further to discover what you really want. Also, try to see yourself through other people's eyes as well as your own. Ultimately, always be optimistic – you never really know what could happen tomorrow. I did three years of the most intense and satisfying training and graduated a qualified, classically trained actress!

Polly (BA Acting, Guildhall School of Music and Drama)

5

Choosing the Right Stuff

Any panel is going to be on the lookout for the three 'T's –
talent, technique and truth. These will show them that you
can be trained and that you have good potential (and that
you are marketable – don't forget there's a tough business
out there). Choosing the right speech and/or song can go a
long way to helping you with this.

What not to choose

There are certain pitfalls in your choice of speech that you
should avoid if you can:

- Be aware that GCSE and A-Level texts are often the
  first port of call for a candidate – with the result that
  the panel can scream inside when speeches from, for
  example, *Road* (Jim Cartwright), *Bouncers* or *Shakers*
  (both by John Godber), or *Like a Virgin* (Gordon
  Steel) are offered yet again, no matter how good these
  plays might be.

- For the same reason, be very careful when using
  monologue compilation books. Whilst these are very
  useful *if* used as a preliminary stepping stone (to
  exploring other plays, for example), they do not feature
  the only plays around, again even if they are good. This
  is even more important if you have not read the whole
  play and do not have any clear idea of vital contextual
  information required to create your character.

- This advice doesn't necessarily apply in the case of
  your Shakespeare speech, though, since every panel

will understand the shortage of pieces (particularly if you are a woman). Simply concentrate on engaging with the character and connecting to the truth – so don't worry about being the third Mariana from *Measure for Measure* that day, for instance. The same requirement to read the entire play does apply, however, for you need to be able to understand the context to make sense of the character.

- Don't choose a monologue (or 'sketch') that was specially written for a particular performer or which doesn't come from a play: a Victoria Wood sketch, for example. The reason for this is that there will be no context and no development of the character or their journey to help you give depth to your audition, and you may be tempted into a caricature rather than a character. Likewise, I would not advise choosing a piece by a very obscure playwright even if the drama school does not actually prohibit this (some do).

- Make sure that there is enough of a serious acting challenge in the speech and the play it is taken from (an adaptation of a fantasy or children's book might not really be appropriate).

- Try to avoid speeches that contain graphic images (like *The Pitchfork Disney* by Philip Ridley, which tells of frying a snake); or has sexual activity requirements (*A Jamaican Airman Foresees His Death* by Fred D'Aguiar); or contains a lot of swearing (*Days of Significance* by Roy Williams). You can edit the bad language out of a speech, however, as long as this does not affect the quality of the character or piece itself.

What to choose

You will want to find the perfect speech that combines rarity of performance with quality of content, but the first thing you must look for is the suitability of the piece for you.

You know you're on to something if you read a speech and are touched by it, can't wait to get to the end of it to see what happens in it, and feel you really 'know' the person who's speaking it – in other words, you are engaging with the material and connecting with the character.

What can help you connect with the character?

- *Your playing age*

  If you are eighteen or nineteen years old, you're looking at a range of approximately five years below your age to five years above, so from about fourteen to twenty-four years of age (depending, always, upon specific individual physical characteristics that would extend or limit your range). This will make the very best use of the life experience you have without highlighting any experience you haven't had.

  What follow are examples of speeches for you to find and read to get into the habit of looking and developing your own eye. This book is not another monologue selection book, rather a workbook to help you develop your search with an educated eye.

  ‣ John Clifford ('Young Clifford') from *Henry VI, Part Two* (Shakespeare): '*Shame and confusion…*' (Act Five Scene Two)

  ‣ The Princess of France from *Love's Labour's Lost* (Shakespeare): '*Good Lord Boyet…*' (Act Two Scene One)

  ‣ Zucco from *Roberto Zucco* (Bernard-Marie Koltes; Methuen): '*I'm just a normal…*'

  ‣ Alice from *Gorgeous* (Anna Furse; Aurora Metro Publications): '*Leonardo – true love…*'

- *Your accent*

  You will study accents at drama school, but for this first audition, it is better in the main to stick with your own accent. So, try to choose a speech for a character from a similar place as yourself, or alternatively, choose a speech that does not demand its own specific accent to make sense of the content. Even though you may be quite proficient, adopting a strange accent can also make you adopt unfamiliar gestures and mannerisms, all of which will disconnect you from the character. With this in mind, you could consider any of the following as a starting point:

▸ Danny from *Blue* (Ursula Rani Sarma; Oberon): '*I lean against the wall...*' (Irish)

▸ Morgan from *The Corn is Green* (Emlyn Williams; Heinemann Educational): '*I shall not need a nail file...*' (Welsh)

▸ Peter from *Toast* (Richard Bean; Oberon): '*Three thousand for Skellies!*' (Yorkshire) (Note that this speech might need editing.)

▸ Martha from *The Letter Box* (Ann Marie di Mambro; Nick Hern Books): '*What...? Who's that?*' (Scots)

▸ Kenny from *An Experienced Woman Gives Advice* (Iain Heggie; Methuen): '*That's why I'm going to tell you...*' (Scots)

• *Your physical type*
Your height, weight and general physical characteristics can sometimes be really useful when choosing a piece. Some examples:

▸ Jo from *Low Level Panic* (Clare McIntyre; Nick Hern Books): '*If I could grow six inches...*'

▸ Moll Cutpurse from *The Roaring Girl* (Middleton and Dekker): '*Oh, here's my gentleman!*' (Act Three Scene One)

• *Your understanding and emotional identification with the character*
Use your own experience and situation positively to strengthen your audition. Examples:

- Bibi from *The Great Celestial Cow* (Sue
  Townsend; Methuen): '*I am twenty years old,
  Hindu…*'(Asian/Midlands)
- Steve from *Flatmates* (Ellen Dryden; First Writes
  Publications): '*What a command of metaphor…*'
  (Student son of wealthy parents)
- Lee from *School Play* (Suzy Almond; Oberon):
  '*Charlie… look at this…*' (Aged fifteen and a bit
  of a lad from a South London comprehensive)

These are not hard and fast rules, but as choosing an inappropriate piece ranks as one of the 'biggest mistakes' that candidates make at their auditions, it makes sense to try hard to get it right.

Extending a speech

You can take several small speeches and cobble them together, making absolutely certain that you do not miss out something important in the character's thoughts or reactions that might be contained in any other character's speech in between, or your character's reaction to them.

Remember, too, that you do not need to have a speech which lasts all of the two (or three) minutes required. As long as the scene is not ridiculously short, a panel will mind less that it is a few seconds short than if you try to present a piece that goes on far longer than they demand.

How to choose

Choosing an audition speech can be tricky given the many, many plays from all genres and periods, but just remember that you are looking for something with which you connect, as well as which fits with the drama school's requirements. This is another reason why you should see as much theatre as you can.

The best advice is not to set out to find a particular speech, but to see and read as much as possible to see what grabs you and makes you want to know more about this character and what happens to them.

Most of the classical texts might be available in your school or from a library. Many are also online, free to access and download. Some of the modern plays may also be in your school library. Alternatively, scour the second-hand bookshops, charity shops and used-book websites like Amazon Marketplace or Abebooks.

In your audition, you have the opportunity to show who you are and what you can do, so it makes good sense to choose a programme of pieces that really contrast, just as you have contrasting qualities.

As you trawl through the plays, keep reminding yourself of:

- All the connections to yourself that you are looking for.
- The requirements of the auditions you are applying for – in terms of period, timing, direct address to the audience, etc.

Your programme

Think of your audition speeches and songs as forming a programme of contrasts that show as much of you as possible (remembering that an ideal song should be considered as part of the whole audition just as much as a speech – see Chapter Seven on musical-theatre auditions).

So, how might a programme work? What follows are two examples to clarify what I mean by 'programme'.

∎

When people speak of you, they describe you as a bright woman, passionate about right and wrong, who is connected to her brain and her emotions. A possible programme for you might start with Portia in *The Merchant of Venice* (Shakespeare).

Portia is a nobleman's daughter. In Act Three Scene Two she is completely taken aback to find herself caring for someone who has to choose the right casket to win her hand in marriage, or leave without her. Normally quite pleased when a potential suitor chooses the wrong casket, she does not want this one (Bassanio) to get it wrong:

> I pray you tarry, pause a day or two
> Before you hazard, for in choosing wrong
> I lose your company: therefore forbear awhile.
> There's something tells me, but it is not love,
> I would not lose you, and you know yourself,
> Hate counsels not in such a quality:
> But lest you should not understand me well –
> And yet a maiden hath no tongue but thought –
> I would detain you here some month or two
> Before you venture for me. I could teach you
> How to choose right, but then I am forsworn.
> So will I never be. So may you miss me.
> But if you do, you'll make me wish a sin,
> That I had been forsworn. Beshrew your eyes.
> They have o'erlooked me and divided me.
> One half of me is yours, the other half yours,
> Mine own, I would say. But if mine, then yours,
> And so all yours. O, these naughty times
> Puts bars between the owners and their rights!
> And so, though yours, not yours. Prove it so,
> Let fortune go to hell for it, not I.
> I speak too long, but 'tis to peise the time,
> To eke it and to draw it out in length.
> To stay you from election.

So, Portia is doing what everyone tries to do – trying to persuade the man she likes to stay with her a bit longer. But the whole thing is complicated by the conditions set in motion by her late father and we see that strong, iron will of hers that comes in so handy later in the play. She will not break the rules to tell him which casket to choose – so you have a delicious mix of desire, thrilling surprise and frustration in this monologue, all wrapped up in cool, clear-eyed honesty and straightforwardness.

See how this contrasts, then, with Rebecca from *Immaculate* (Oliver Lansley; Nick Hern Books). *Immaculate* is a modern take on the story of the immaculate conception. In this scene, from Act Two, Rebecca has come to explain and apologise to her friend Mia for going out with Mia's ex:

> Hi... Look, there's something I have to say. I probably should have told you earlier, but I didn't know if it was going anywhere but now I think it is, or thought it was, but now you're pregnant, so I probably shouldn't tell you anyway 'cause stress is bad for the baby, not that you're keeping it, right? God, you're huge, are those my boots...?
>
> Look... Michael and I are together...
>
> We're a couple, I'm sorry I didn't tell you, I didn't plan it, I was out and saw Michael and said hello and we got talking and it came out that he'd always quite fancied me but couldn't do anything about it obviously 'cause we were best mates and I said I quite fancied him too, which was why I was sometimes a bit of a bitch towards him because I think subconsciously I fancied him and I always used to talk to Ed about him and that's why Ed never wanted to come out with us in a foursome because he thought I fancied Michael which I didn't, or didn't think I did, but turns out I did, because I fancy him now, anyway, we weren't going to do anything because you two had just broken up and I knew how pissed off you'd be but then we said, well, maybe we should just have a kiss, while we're both single then, just to get it out of our systems, so we had a kiss, and then the kiss carried on, and things and things and we ended up having sex, which I'm not proud of but it was good, but it was bad because the condom broke and I had to get the morning-after pill,

> which was fucking awful and I was terrified 'cause I
> thought I was gonna have a baby... but now you tell me
> that you're pregnant and you say that you haven't had
> sex with anyone since Michael, which means he must be
> the father but you don't want to tell me because I made
> such a fuss... when he dumped you. Which means you're
> lying to me and he's lying to me, and I'm lying to you...
> and I'm going to lose my best friend and my boyfriend,
> not that I call him my boyfriend but technically he is, and
> I'll be helpless and hopeless and friendless and loveless
> and die old and alone with thread veins and bladder
> weakness and a houseful of cats...

Who would not be nervous and guilty and excited all at once to be in this position? It is important that you do not give way to caricature or 'funny' acting here. If you are sincere and connected then the speech will work for itself, and the programme of Portia and Rebecca could work very well. They are both interesting women who deal with their problems in different ways, both characters accessible in situation and personality to a 'bright' woman who is 'passionate about right and wrong'.

■

Here's another example of a programme:

You're a bit of a party animal, loving whiling away the hours with friends and putting all thoughts of responsibility on the back burner. So let's have a look at Prince Hal in Act Four Scene Two of *Henry IV, Part Two*. Heir to the throne, Hal has rushed to the deathbed of his father, the King, only to make the mistake of thinking that he is too late – but the King has just fallen asleep. Hal (who has been so irresponsible up to now that the country he is about to assume the throne of believes him to be a hedonist) took the crown from his father's head and left the room in turmoil. He now has to come back to face an ear-bashing from his father and this is his response (it may be necessary for this speech to be edited, depending on the time you are allowed):

O, pardon me, my liege! But for my tears,
The moist impediments unto my speech,
I had forestalled this dear and deep rebuke
Ere you with grief had spoke and I had heard
The course of it so far. There is your crown,
And He that wears the crown immortally
Long guard it yours! If I affect it more
Than as your honour and as your renown,
Let me no more from this obedience rise,
Which my most true and inward duteous spirit
Teacheth, this prostrate and exterior bending.
Heaven witness with me, when I here came in,
And found no course of breath within your majesty,
How cold it struck my heart! If I do feign,
O, let me in my present wildness die
And never live to show the incredulous world
The noble change that I have purposed!
Coming to look on you, thinking you dead –
And dead, almost, my liege, to think you were –
I spake unto this crown as having sense,
And thus upbraided it: 'The care on thee depending
Hath fed upon the body of my father;
Therefore thou best of gold art worst of gold;
Other, less fine in carat, is more precious,
Preserving life in medicine potable;
But thou, most fine, most honoured, most renowned,
Hast eat thy bearer up.' Thus, my royal liege,
Accusing it, I put it on my head,
To try with it, as with an enemy
That had before my face murdered my father,
The quarrel of a true inheritor.
But if it did infect my blood with joy,
Or swell my thoughts to any strain of pride,
If any rebel or vain spirit of mine
Did with the least affection of a welcome
Give entertainment to the might of it,
Let heaven forever keep it from my head,
And make me as the poorest vassal is
That doth with awe and terror kneel to it!

You have a number of acting choices in this scene, but it is accessible enough in terms of the parent/child relationship at the very least. Now, see how this monologue might marry with one of Valya's from Scene Three of *Playing the Victim* (The Presnyakov Brothers; Nick Hern Books). *Playing the Victim* is a complex play, a satire on the violence in everyday life. The play centres on Valya, a student who drops out of university to get himself a job. And that job happens to be playing the victim in police crime-scene reconstructions. The cycle of events that he has to participate in highlights the brutality of contemporary life – even down to the murder of the Inspector who employs him (with the use of a fugu fish) in a restaurant. The following speech may also need to be edited for time:

> I was always good at thinking up ways to get out of things. From when I was a kid, I never did anything I didn't want to. And not because I was lazy... That's not the reason, or at least that's a reason, but there's something else deeper which makes me lazy. I think it's fear. Sometimes I'm afraid just to go out in the street. I'm afraid to go for bread, or take a walk. And then comes the laziness... Maybe, if you could find out, you might find that there's a reason for fear, as well... Still, I've stopped being scared of everything that used to scare me because I can think of ways to get out of everything. Even in school, in junior school, when they started taking us to the swimming pool and I was scared of water – my mum almost drowned when she was young, that was before I was born, so it must be that it carried through to me... I mean, her fear of drowning was carried through to me, although she was a good swimmer actually, and even after she almost drowned she didn't stop swimming – but I can't stand water, deep rivers, seas... I never go in – not even to my knees... I don't like crossing bridges either. And in school, when they started taking us to the swimming pool for P.E., I just didn't take my swimming trunks with me and they wouldn't let me into the swimming pool,

because according to the rules you couldn't go swimming in the same pants you were wearing for hygiene reasons, although I suppose you could have been walking around in clean pants anyway... But they didn't take into account that people could be walking around during the day in clean pants. Or I suppose you could take swimming trunks, but dirty ones, and give everyone a nasty little dose of something. Anyway, I never took my trunks, I used to pretend I'd forgotten. They told me off, but never gave me a detention and I pretended I really wanted to go swimming and I begged them to let me in in the pants I was wearing... But they didn't let me and they thought they were punishing me like that. By the way, if people think you're being punished as it is, they never punish you any more... Yeah...

I think most teenagers could relate to Valya and the way he reacts to his problems!

■

So now you're thinking of a programme, instead of a random speech and song. But the two examples above are just to get you thinking of connecting what you are like to what a character is like, to help you engage with what you're doing.

The following are to prompt you into more 'pick 'n' mixing' to find the best programme for you:

Female monologues

- Are you a tough character, vengeful in frustration? Then have a look at Queen Isabella from *Edward II* by Shakespeare's contemporary Christopher Marlowe. Queen Isabella has had to put up with being humiliated by her husband Edward, and his male lover Gaveston. Appealing to him has had no effect and when the lovers go out, her speech continues and she shows us exactly what she's thinking about her situation. The speech is in Act One Scene Four: '*Wherein, my lord, have I deserv'd those words?*'

- If asked, would you say you were a fairly serious-minded, sincere individual? If so, then the Princess of France from Shakespeare's *Love's Labour's Lost* might be right for you. The Princess represents truth and straightforwardness in this play, and highlights the important things in life as opposed to artificial frivolity. Look at '*Good lord Boyet, my beauty, though but mean*', her response to her attendant Boyet's flattery of her (Act Two Scene One). When news of her father's death is delivered, she tells the King (her proposed suitor) that she will only accept his proposal if he goes into a barren hermitage for a year, allowing her that same time to mourn her father: '*A time methinks too short. To make a world without end bargain in...*' (Act Five Scene Two).

- Perhaps people would hesitate to speak out of turn to you, since they know you as a loyal and grounded friend who will speak your mind no matter what? Then Emilia from *Othello* might be an appropriate choice for you to consider. In the speech beginning '*But I do think it is their husbands' faults...*' (Act Four Scene Three), she defends women's behaviour when they are badly treated by their husbands. It is performed quite regularly, but is good and offers a great deal of scope for making your own mark. Do not worry that it seems shorter than others for there is such an interesting thought-path through it, with Emilia's running commentary taking in her friend's situation as well as her own.

Try reading the following and considering how you would engage with these characters:

- Lady Anne from *Richard III* (Shakespeare): '*No? Why? When he that is my husband now…*' (Act Four Scene One)

- Luciana from *The Comedy of Errors* (Shakespeare): '*And may it be that you have quite forgot…*' (Act Three Scene Two) (This is performed quite regularly, so be strong with your connections to it.)

- Joan la Pucelle (Joan of Arc) from *Henry VI, Part One* (Shakespeare): '*The Regent conquers and the Frenchmen fly…*' (Act Five Scene Three)

- Innogen from *Cymbeline* (Shakespeare): '*Who, thy lord? That is my lord Leonatus?*' (Act Three Scene Two) (This will need some editing.) Or: '*I see a man's life is a tedious one…*' (Act Three Scene Six)

- Vittoria from *The White Devil* (John Webster): '*A house of convertites, what's that?*' (Act Three Scene Two) (This speech must be put together by editing other people's interjections.)

- Duchess from *The Duchess of Malfi* (John Webster): '*Farewell Cariola…*' (Act Four Scene Two) (This speech needs editing for continuity.)

- Agnes from *Agnes of God* (John Pielmeier; Samuel French Inc.): '*Where do you think babies come from?*' (Act One Scene Four). Or: '*Why are you crying?*' (Act Two Scene Four)

- Manon from *Manon/Sandra* (Michel Tremblay; Nick Hern Books): There is a wide choice of audition possibilities in this play (since there are only two characters who do not talk directly to each other), so it will depend on which aspect of Manon's conversation with the audience that you engage with the most.

- Joan from *The Lark* (Jean Anouilh; Methuen): '*You see simply…*' to '*…a born leader, Robert.*' (Part One). Or: '*But I am ill-bred…*' to '*…Joan is herself again!*' (Part Two)

- The Audition (Girl) from *The Good Doctor* (Neil Simon; Samuel French Ltd): '*I would like to do…*'
- Sheila from *An Inspector Calls* (J.B. Priestley; Penguin): '*You knew it was me…*' (Act One)

Male monologues

- Maybe people would call you a bit arrogant or cocky? If so, you might want to explore Lewis the Dauphin from *King John*, a macho young man who doesn't like being told what to do. Look at his speech beginning '*Your grace shall pardon me, I will not back…*' (Act Five Scene Two), which might give you some fun.

- Have you ever made a miscalculation that someone else has taken advantage of? Did this result in you feeling sorry for yourself, worried about the outcome and forced to think about a serious, bigger picture? Then you might want to consider Claudio's speech in *Measure for Measure* beginning '*Ay, but to die, and go we know not where…*' (Act Three Scene One).

Here are some other monologue examples to get you thinking about your personal connection to the characters:

- Berowne from *Love's Labour's Lost* (Shakespeare): '*Thus pour the stars down plagues for perjury…*' (Act Five Scene Two). Or: '*And I, forsooth, in love!*' (Act Three Scene Two)
- Antipholus of Syracuse from *The Comedy of Errors* (Shakespeare): '*Sweet Mistress – what your name is else, I know not…*' (Act Three Scene Two)
- Rumour from *Henry IV, Part Two* (Shakespeare): '*Open your ears; for which of you will stop…*' (Prologue)
- Morton from *Henry IV, Part Two* (Shakespeare): '*I am sorry I should force you to believe…*' (Act One Scene One)

- Proteus from *The Two Gentlemen of Verona* (Shakespeare): *'To leave my Julia… shall I be forsworn?'* (Act Two Scene Seven) (This speech needs editing.)

- Edward II from *Edward II* (Christopher Marlowe) – *'Leicester, if gentle words might comfort me…'* (Act Five Scene One)

- Ferdinand from *The Duchess of Malfi* (John Webster): *'Whate'er thou art that hast enjoy'd my sister…'* (Act Three Scene Two)

- Flamineo from *The White Devil* (John Webster): *'Th'art a noble sister…'* (Act Five Scene Six)

- Cusins from *Major Barbara* (George Bernard Shaw): *'It is not the sale…'*

- Gerald from *A Woman of No Importance* (Oscar Wilde): *'Dear mother, I am afraid…'* (Act Three) (This speech needs editing.)

- Tanner from *Man and Superman* (George Bernard Shaw; Penguin): *'…you, Tavy, are an artist…'* (Act One)

- The Prince from *Leocadia* (Jean Anouilh; Methuen): *'Sit down…'* (Scene Four) (Editing out Amanda's line.)

- Elliot from *Taking Breath* (Sarah Daniels; Faber and Faber): *'Would you look at them?'* (Scene Two)

- Ronin from *Discontented Winter: House Remix* (Bryony Lavery; Faber and Faber): *'Now's not a good time…'* (Opening)

Obviously, there is an entire world of plays out there for you to explore, and many anthologies of monologue speeches. Bear in mind the aforementioned warnings about using these. For example, if there's a good speech for you in a monologue book then read the whole play to check if this character is really good for you or to see if there's another speech possibility that may suit you. Better yet, has that playwright written any other plays that might give you even more opportunity?

It's vital that you bear in mind all the elements discussed above in respect of your age, accent, physical type, etc. Do not choose a speech that forces you into acting choices that are unnatural for you. For example, there are many good plays by Oscar Wilde and George Bernard Shaw, but a candidate can make huge mistakes in opting for 'style' over content, which disconnects them from the truth of the character and situation in a welter of accents and mannerisms.

It is sometimes easier to choose the classical speech first, since there will be much more leeway in contemporary pieces from which to choose your contrasting piece. There are not many comedic classical pieces in verse, for example (and keep referring to the audition requirements to make sure that you are complying with timing restrictions as well as periods and types).

Remember that a good speech is one that resonates with you and where you identify with the character and understand their experience. Don't choose a speech deliberately to shock, that has gratuitous swearing in it or gross sexual content because the chances are the panel will be repelled, not surprised into submission. You can edit a speech as long as it retains what you find exciting in it, as well as the logical emotional process.

Looking for speeches

Obviously, all the theatre productions you see can give you ideas for speeches. For example, each year the National Theatre mounts a series of specially commissioned plays for sixteen- to nineteen-year-olds called NT Connections. You can see the productions and the plays are all published in a single volume (by Faber and Faber). These may also be in your school or local library.

Summary

- Put together a programme of pieces and songs which you are strongly connected to and which comply with the school's requirements.

Practical

- See and read as much as you can!
- Remembering the warnings, see the Appendix for some monologue/audition anthologies to start you off.

6

Working It!

If you have judiciously begun your preparations by the time you start applying to drama schools, then you will almost certainly have enhanced your ability to make the most of your chances:

- You will have begun to listen to and watch yourself more objectively in performance, and started to build and improve upon your skills base with singing and vocal work, dance classes and/or fitness exercises.

- You will have developed a clear understanding of what you want from your training in accordance with the business, your abilities and objectives, and you will have begun to develop your own critical eye from all the plays and musicals that you have seen.

- You will have thoroughly researched the schools to draw up your shortlist.

- You will have attended open days at those schools and noted the atmosphere as supportive to your needs – you may also have one of their holiday courses under your belt.

- You will have been an audience member at one or more final showcases, making notes on the performances and productions of these third-year graduate students – did they handle the classical text with good vocal skills and was there rich meaning in their interpretation, for example? You may even have picked up CVs of the actors, to note how these are put together and to see what work the students did in their three years at drama school – and who directed them.

It might also give you an inkling as to the agents they've signed with.

- You will have familiarised yourself with the ethos and approach of the schools on your shortlist as well as their audition requirements.

- You will have the right genre and number of audition pieces, selected because you connect with them:

  ▸ You were excited by them, couldn't wait to see what happened to the characters, and you think they're saying something worth hearing.

  ▸ You have things in common with the character that personalises them to you – age, background, experience, etc.

  ▸ You can instinctively tune into the scene.

  ▸ You've read the plays that your speeches come from and have begun to ask yourself all the questions you need to answer in your preparation of the character.

  ▸ The pieces (and songs) comprise an interesting programme for you that shows your strengths.

Now you can really begin to work on your pieces, to prepare in depth.

Your working process

To be an actor you need to develop huge curiosity about your world, the people in it and you need to be curious about *you*! You are the unique element that you will bring to a character, so the better you observe yourself and your life, the more you'll have to use. You'll also be in a better position to work out what your specific strengths and weaknesses are.

This curiosity is sharpened by the observation of all that's around you – so next time you're at the gym or swimming pool, sitting in a library, café or park, just spend some time watching other people. What do you see in their faces?

What clues about their lives or their state of mind can you see in their posture, the way they walk, or in the pace of their movement? How is what they do being affected by the fact of being in public?

Make your eyes and ears work for you. Watch plays and films to develop your curiosity and make you question how other actors have observed and made their choices.

Curiosity will help you to take your acting seriously and embrace the ongoing process of the craft. Acting grows and changes, like life. It isn't a passive art form.

Convincing other people starts by convincing yourself. Every audition panel is looking to see if what you do is coming from your own 'belief'. This is your 'centre'.

What follows is a short exploration of just one of the many paths you can take towards this connecting and 'believing'. Take from it what you need. We'll start with an imaginary website to get you in the right place:

WWW.THETIMEANDTHEPLACE.COM

First of all, the www stands for WHO?, WHAT?, WHY? Let's look at each of these questions in turn.

WHO?

You know your name, address and the school you went to; who brought you up and the rules you were brought up with; you have moments from your life that stand out for you – happy or sad – that make you smile the moment you think of them, bring tears to your eyes or make you squirm with embarrassment; you have achievements – sporting or academic; you have dreams, hopes and aspirations, some of which you will never tell to another soul. Write down all of these facts and memories, in a diary or blog-type journal if that works for you. Awareness of yourself will enhance your awareness of your character.

Now look at your character in the same way, working out – using facts in the play and your own imagination – about their life. It's worth writing down all your discoveries and decisions so you can refer to them later. Stage directions may give you some information about the character, but are they the words of the playwright or just the decisions made by the first company who put the show on? For example, George Bernard Shaw wrote wonderful and detailed introductions to his plays, and lengthy stage directions, so if you are playing Joan from *Saint Joan* or Fanny from *Fanny's First Play* you will have a first-rate source of information.

What does your character say about him or herself? What choices does your character make in the play? How does your scene fit into the picture of his or her journey? For example, look at the opening, prologue speech by the Earl of Rochester from *The Libertine* (Stephen Jeffreys; Nick Hern Books), which begins: '*Allow me to be frank at the commencement: you will not like me.*' What does this say about the character, how he wants to be viewed, and how he views himself?

What do the other characters say about your character? The opinions of others can be very revealing, but it's worth mentioning that characters do not always give a balanced picture about one another or themselves. They may even be lying, which is why you need to read the whole play.

WHAT?

What are *you* at this audition for? To gain a place at drama school – and that's your overriding goal, the big picture. Everything you do is to achieve that end – from buying this book, to taking classes, reading plays, etc., etc. You can see from this list that there are many 'mini' goals that are all stepping stones on the path to that big one.

And your character is the same, doing what they do (and choosing how and when they do it) to get what they want. What does your character want overall in the play? So how does this scene fit into the big picture? This is the reason your character is here.

For example, does he or she want to make someone do something? Do they want to hurt someone? Or do they perhaps want to be comforted because they're frightened? For example, Eva from *Kindertransport* (Diane Samuels; Nick Hern Books): '*Mutti! Vati! Hello! Hello!*'

Does your character change his or her mini-goals as the scene progresses because what they want becomes more important to them? For example, Michael from *Immaculate* (Oliver Lansley; Nick Hern Books): '*I don't believe this, how did this happen?*'

Once you know what your character wants, you can then work out what your character does to get it: this is your '*action*'. For example, 'I want to "stop" her from telling on me.' Of course, there are many different ways to 'stop' someone from doing something so it might involve lying to her, or you might have to distract her, or you might just grab on to her physically! For example, look at *Be My Baby* (Amanda Whittington; Nick Hern Books). The year is 1964 and the setting is a Church of England mother and baby home. In Scene Six, Mary (a nineteen-year-old who is seven months pregnant) is on the telephone to a prospective employer. See how her choices alter in the speech beginning '*Hello, Mrs Wilson…*'. How would you use the dynamic of the character at the other end of the telephone to help you?

WHY?

You need to work out why what your character wants is so important to them, so you can understand why they do what they do to get it.

For example, if you don't mind whether you have a pink sweet or a red one, you aren't going to pursue either one very passionately – because it won't matter. However, how will it change your game plan if you *really* want a red sweet? What about if the person who has the sweets will not let you have the red one because they know you want it? In other words, what you *do* to get the sweet matters more.

How far is your character willing to go to get what they want? Focus on 'What is going to happen here if I don't get what I want?' This will help you to make your action clear. Does your character give up? No – because it's important for them to get what they want (or it would be a dull play). So there's a problem they need to solve in some way and you must identify their choice of solution.

Often, the really interesting part of a drama are the obstacles that get in the way of the character getting what they want. Just as in life other characters' objectives may get in the way.

One method to help you clarify what your character wants is to work out what their unspoken thoughts are – the running commentary of their thought processes. Everyone has a commentary in their head all the time. When you're hearing your own character's commentary, tune into the running commentary of any other present character (even though you aren't part of that conversation!).

In other words, you need to be 'listening' not only to what they're actually saying, but to what they're thinking, too. These running commentaries will help you see what's driving the scene – and your character. For example, look at Valmont from *Les Liaisons Dangereuses* (Laclos adapted by Christopher Hampton; Faber and Faber). Valmont's running commentary in Act Two Scene Six is very interesting!

Whatever your goal and however important it is to your character, take care if what your character is doing to achieve their goal is completely out of your own nature and experience. For example, your character hates someone enough to assault them, yet you (fortunately!) have never been in this position.

In moments like this, you may sometimes have to use your imagination to find a similar example as a substitution to ensure you will always connect to your own truthful feelings and the ways in which you express them. This will help prevent you from 'pretending' an emotion. All 'pretending' does is make you 'act' on the surface, disconnected from the truth, and no one (including yourself) will 'believe' you as the character.

In the example of your character hating someone and assaulting them, the first thing that would disconnect you from your truthful feelings would be to play 'hate'; it would make the speech utterly superficial. You could try, instead, to think of something that has given you cause to react with anger, annoyance and disgust – being 'eaten alive' by some persistent mosquito might do it!

And, however important your goal is to you, avoid disconnecting yourself from the truth by slavishly following stage directions. These might make you do something that is completely out of your ken, that you cannot even find a good substitution to help you with, and will not work for you in audition.

For example, don't 'scream hysterically' if this is the stage direction but is something you never have done (and never would). Remember – for others to 'believe', you must believe.

You are here to show the panel the wonderful raw talent, the rough diamond that you are! You are auditioning for some of the best drama schools in the world, and they have the experience to take your talent and give you the tools to develop it.

Before they'll offer you a place, however, they'll need to see what talent you have for 'believing'. That is your goal for the audition. Another of the big mistakes that candidates make is to become disconnected from the truth so that they stop believing in the moment and they become inflexible (in other words: 'This is what I've practised so this is what I do'). Instant acting. These disconnected choices are so polished and exaggerated that when the panel tries to work with them to get them to open up and find that truth again, the candidate can't do it.

THETIMEANDTHEPLACE

So, you know WHO?, WHAT? and WHY? – what about the time and the place in which your scenes are happening?

For audition purposes, only use such information to fill in the gaps for you and help you to 'believe' instead of demonstrating. For example, a stage direction of 'sitting round a campfire' should help you envisage and imagine, not so you can rub your arms and pretend to be cold!

COM

The COM part of this website of the imagination refers to the playwright, the director, other actors in your scene, and your audience (in the case of a performance).

As far as an audition is concerned, it also refers to the panel and any of them, or the current students, who may work with you during your audition.

You must be aware of how you are COMmunicating the character, the speech and the ideas within it to your audience, and how effectively you draw them into your world. It is an act of collaboration in which you are developing a COMplicity, a shared understanding, between yourself and the audience.

Do not forget the COM, because it can also go a long way to helping you remain connected to the truth of the moment.

WWW.THETIMEANDTHEPLACE.COM: an example
(Iachimo from *Cymbeline* by Shakespeare)

WHO *is he?*

You've chosen a speech that resonates with you – that you connect with. The character fits your age range; he's well-educated and clever. When you read the speech you were intrigued by him and what he was doing.

In this example, he is Iachimo (pronounced Yak-ee-mo) from Shakespeare's *Cymbeline.* He's a young nobleman (Italian, but doesn't speak with an accent or have any modern 'cod-European' characteristics). He's also quite cunning and likes making mischief, which is what attracted you to him in the first place. He belongs to the type of characters referred to as 'Machiavellian', which are really characterised by their deceitful natures. Iago (from *Othello*) is a Machiavellian character and some people believe that the name Iachimo might come from Iago (i.e. 'little Iago').

WHAT *does he want in this scene?*

Iachimo has come to England from Rome, as a result of having made a bet with a banished English gentleman (Posthumus). Posthumus maintains that his wife (Innogen, in some editions of the play called Imogen, the daughter of King Cymbeline) is the most faithful woman. Iachimo makes the bet that he can take Innogen's honour.

Innogen will have nothing to do with him, however, so in order to win the bet he has tricked her into taking a trunk full of his valuable things into her bedroom for safe keeping. In reality he has hidden in the trunk for hours waiting until she's asleep in bed before creeping out of his hiding place. He takes various notes of her bedroom and even of her body, finishing with stealing a bracelet from her arm, all as 'evidence' of Innogen's infidelity that he will use to win the bet.

WHY *is this important to him?*

Iachimo is a cynic who likes to indulge himself. He judges everyone by his own cynical standards (especially women), but his cynicism may simply be a measure of self-defence and this bet might be needed by him to preserve intact his way of looking at the world. After all, if he isn't right about Innogen, his whole philosophy of life and people becomes suspect. On a different level, a bet's a bet and Shakespeare raises the stakes in this way to motivate Iachimo into doing what he is doing. He has just bet Posthumus 10,000 ducats (a fortune at the time), so quite a lot is riding on this.

A clue to the running commentary and inner reality of the character, and to the problems he has to overcome, lies in the fact that he is completely overwhelmed by the beauty of Innogen and also in the fact that at the end of the play he is filled with remorse at his actions, confessing what he has done. So read the play, or you will miss important characteristics for you to connect with!

THE TIME AND THE PLACE

Iachimo is hiding in a trunk in a princess's bedroom in the middle of the night and in a country far away from his own. You really don't need to be in a box though! You could begin standing upstage or even offstage, if you feel this is more comfortable. Alternatively, you could just crouch to begin.

You do need to place Innogen, however. Where should her bed be? How high is it? How much room is there around it? Where are the walls, the window, the arras, her arm with the bracelet on it, the book (although you do not need to place this if you cut this small section of the speech). When all's said and done, if you 'see' Innogen and her bedroom, then so will your audience.

You do not need to have any props at all – and while we're on the subject of props, be very careful when you include them. In the main, they are not necessary. The panel is analysing your belief and the truth of what you're engaging with – you will learn the techniques you need for working with props at drama school, so leave them until then or you may be thrown by the props or create an unnecessary distraction for the panel.

And for the time of day? It is in the middle of the night – but do not whisper the speech! You can begin by speaking more softly, but Shakespeare has given you a lot of help that means you can speak clearly.

COM

The important thing is that you have in your imagination a complete picture of the room and of the other character 'onstage', so that you can communicate the truth of the scene with full belief.

When this happens, you will feel Shakespeare's hand supporting you in the small of your back, and there will be truth in Iachimo's reactions to the sleeping Innogen. The timing of the asides will help you establish complicity with the audience/panel.

Be prepared for someone to play the part of Innogen. Having the physical presence of someone to respond to can be hugely helpful, but if this does not happen, go with the flow of your own imagination.

And now, let's look at the speech itself (from Act Two Scene Two):

> The crickets sing, and man's o'er-laboured sense
> Repairs itself by rest. Our Tarquin thus
> Did softly press the rushes, ere he wakened

The chastity he wounded. Cytherea,
How bravely thou becom'st thy bed: fresh lily,
And whiter than the sheets: that I might touch,
But kiss, one kiss! Rubies unparagoned,
How dearly they do't! 'Tis her breathing that
Perfumes the chamber thus: the flame o'th'taper
Bows toward her, and would underpeep her lids
To see th'enclosed lights, now canopied
Under these windows, white and azure laced
With blue of heaven's own tinct. But my design:
To note the chamber. I will write all down.
Such and such pictures, there the window, such
Th'adornment of her bed: the arras, figures,
Why, such and such: and the contents o'th'story.
Ah, but some natural notes about her body,
Above ten thousand meaner movables
Would serve t'enrich mine inventory.
O sleep, thou ape of death, lie dull upon her,
And be her sense but as a monument
Thus in a chapel lying. Come off, come off;
As slippery as the Gordian knot was hard.
'Tis mine, and this will witness outwardly,
As strongly as the conscience does within,
To th'madding of her lord. On her left breast
A mole, cinque-spotted: like the crimson drops
I'th'bottom of a cowslip. Here's a voucher
Stronger than ever law could make; this secret
Will force him think I have picked the lock and ta'en
The treasure of her honour. No more: to what end?
Why should I write this down that's riveted,
Screwed to my memory? She hath been reading late,
The tale of Tereus. Here the leaf's turned down
Where Philomel gave up. I have enough.
To th'trunk again, and shut the spring of it.
Swift, swift, you dragons of the night, that dawning
May bare the raven's eye! I lodge in fear:
Though this a heavenly angel, hell is here.
One, two, three: time, time!

Initial notes

So, you've read the speech through. First impressions? Here are some initial notes to help:

- The original performance would have taken place in broad daylight and with little set, so Shakespeare is giving you some good 'stage directions' within the spoken text here.

- Iachimo is getting out of the trunk, so there is more stage action required here (to interpret as is appropriate for your performance).

- How stunned is Iachimo by the sight of Innogen?

- Would Iachimo risk a kiss? Or is he just talking about one of her lips kissing the other? It's up to you to interpret, bearing in mind the danger of the situation and Iachimo's character.

- How beautiful is this poetry? And what does it say about Iachimo?

- Iachimo has to wrench himself away to get on with the task in hand (this refers to the problems he has to overcome to get what he wants).

- See how Iachimo turns away to make his notes, then is drawn back to her.

- Remember the danger to Iachimo as he pulls the bracelet off Innogen's arm.

- Does he lose patience with himself? Or is he triumphant? Or something else? You have to choose.

- How important does something have to be to be 'screwed to my memory'?

Your own words

Now you're starting to imagine the scene, it might be an idea to put the speech into your own words (in modern English) and as simply as possible so that you have total mastery of its sense. For example:

It's late – so quiet I can hear the crickets singing.

Everyone's in bed.

Tarquin stepped on Lucrece's carpet like this, just before he woke her up and raped her.

Oh Venus, how gorgeous you are in your bed, pure as a lily and just as pale.

I wish I could touch you.

Just kiss you. One kiss. Your lips are like perfect rubies; how perfectly they kiss each other/me.

Her breath is like perfume in here.

The candle flame is attracted towards her, wanting to see the heavenly blue eyes through her translucent eyelids.

But I've got to get on and make notes about the room.

I'll write everything down – the pictures, the window, the bedclothes, the tapestry, the carvings in the bedpost and the story in them.

But some personal notes about her body would be much better proof than 10,000 notes about furniture.

Oh, let her sleep so deeply that she's like a statue in a chapel.

Come on! Come on! This bracelet's as hard to get off as the legendary Gordian knot was to untie.

Ah – got you. And this will be as good as knowing she's been unfaithful would be to make her husband crazy.

On her left breast, a five-spotted mole, like a cowslip: this is the strongest proof ever. This private detail will force him to believe I've slept with her.

No more! What's the point?

I don't need to write this down, it's branded on my mind.

She's been reading the story of Tereus and has got to the part where Philomel surrenders.

I have enough.

Get back in the trunk and shut the lid.

Come on, morning. I'm terrified.

She may be an angel – but this is hell, not heaven.

One, two, three. Time, time.

Before you forget that your own words are not Shakespeare's, you need now to go back to the speech and make sure you can convey the same sense in the actual verse.

Verse-speaking

When a speech is in verse, it's a heightened way of expressing something, but don't panic and think that you must put on a special 'voice' to speak it. Instead, allow the genius of Shakespeare to do the work for you in the audition:

- See how he has given you the 's' sounds to help you with the fact that Iachimo is whispering (so you don't have to).

- Look at the way in which the punctuation helps you with the phrasing and thought processes. When you're rehearsing the scene:

  ‣ Read through the speech out loud and only to the first punctuation mark you get to.

  ‣ Stop speaking and (silently) walk across the room in a different direction, thinking of the thought you have just expressed with that phrase, then stop again.

  ‣ Read to the next punctuation point and think about the step in logic, the progression between the last thought and this one.

▸ Repeat this reading/walking pattern throughout
the speech.

What information do the thoughts give you? Is it to do with
WHO? For example, the classical references tell you about his
education. Or WHAT? For example, the harder sound of the
'But' following the softer 'tinct' reminds the character and
us of what he's here for. Or WHY? For example, the prayer
to 'sleep', the 'fear' reference, and the shorter phrases
(sounding breathless) remind us of the importance of his
objective to him and also of the problems he's facing. Or do
they give clues to THETIMEANDTHEPLACE? Look at the 'stage
directions' embedded in the text. How does this information help the COM? For example, the rhetorical questions
give some help with the relationship between the character,
the sleeping Innogen and the audience.

How does each thought connect to the last and the next?
Remember that a thought may be connected to another
much further on, or going back in the speech, as well.

See also how Shakespeare's choice of words helps you to
connect to the character within yourself. For example, why
do the crickets 'sing' and Tarquin 'softly' 'press' the rushes?
Why 'note' then 'write' then 'riveted'? Why 'lodge'? You need
to think carefully about every word that Shakespeare has
carefully and purposefully selected.

You should have a good few ideas at this point, which
means you must read the whole play to help you with the
acting choices that are coming up.

Further exercises

The work you do with a speech should help to strengthen
your connection to the character, the truth and the
'moment' (all of which is designed to help you believe). It
is to re-establish the WWW.THETIMEANDTHEPLACE.COM. For
example:

- WHO?
  'Hotseat' the character (asking yourself questions that you answer in character) based on your research, examining what Iachimo thinks and says about himself, and what other characters say about him to connect you to him.

- WHAT?
  Thought-track the speech (discovering your running commentary) to keep bringing you back to Iachimo's goal in the scene.

- WHY?
  Substitute the character's situation for one that is real from your own life, to get closer to why Iachimo is doing what he's doing, and why his goals are so important to him.

Learning the lines

By this stage you should have at least a good working knowledge of your lines, since you will have combed through the speech so much.

But all your work up to this point will have kept the character 'on the page' so that you can establish your strong lines of connection. You will have been going back to the speech, looking for clues so often that you will (hopefully) avoid the 'let's pretend' game with the emotions.

Consequently, your acting choices (why, how and when you say and do what you do) will remain flexible and open to all the possibilities there are on the day of the audition. You will not be frozen into one particular choice, but will be able to stay connected to the truth, and the 'moment' and the belief will happen for you (and, therefore, the panel).

In other words, the character will *exist* and you will not be caught 'acting' or playing false, superficial emotions. You will effectively 'recreate' the moment each time you do it.

WWW.THETIMEANDTHEPLACE.COM: another example
(Shirley from *Jordan* by Anna Reynolds with Moira
Buffini; Nick Hern Books)

Now let's turn to a modern speech to see how the process
might help with that. Again, you've chosen something that
resonates with you and your experience.

WHO *is she?*

Shirley is in her early twenties. When she was nineteen she
started a relationship with a man who abused her (physically and mentally) and fathered her child. He was not
interested in the little boy (Jordan) until he had left Shirley
and taken up with another woman, at which point he
applied for custody of Jordan. Shirley is driven to despair
and she kills her baby and tries to take her own life. Failing
to do so, she finds herself on trial.

WHAT *does she want in this speech?*

Let's look at the speech itself so we can work out Shirley's
goals:

> Every time I hear... Every time I hear a baby cry on the
> wing below me, every time I see a woman kissing her
> baby's head or sucking its toes or blowing on its soft, fat
> stomach, my throat sticks hard and rasping and I can't
> swallow. I freeze when I hear wailing; the crying of a child
> tears me into tiny pieces. I curl myself into a ball as small
> and tight as I can and move away from the noise. I want
> to comfort that crying child. Davey used to say to me:
> 'You smother that kid. You love him too much. It's not
> normal.' Oh, he was right, wasn't he?
>
> ['If the victim had been under twelve months of age, my
> client would have been charged with infanticide. As the
> victim was just thirteen months old, she must be tried
> for murder. I ask to consider how unfit the woman you

see before you is to undergo the torture of a life sentence in prison. She should be free to walk from this court today, to pick up the pieces of her life and one day know the joy of bearing other children... ' Ha.]

I walk very near to the edge of the cliffs and look down. They're all worn away by the tide. 'Erosion,' said the wise old man. 'They can only take so much and then they begin to crumble.' Waves of pain pass, breaking over my head, and I wait and I hurt less, and I think maybe it gets easier with time! Then I see a downy head, or hear a gurgle, a small fat hand reaching out, and the cliffs begin to crumble.

But now it's time to go. Jordan? One thing or the other now. A life sentence or freedom.

Freedom.

Firstly, the section in square brackets is left in for your contextual information – you do not need these lines in your speech so they can be cut, leaving the thought-path intact. But look how the information contained in those lines deepens your knowledge of both the situation and Shirley's reactions (particularly the sardonic 'Ha' at the end).

When linked to the last few lines of the speech, we can see that Shirley's goal is connected to the sentence she receives. What she wants is 'Freedom.' But consider carefully all the possibilities of the phrase 'A life sentence' and how it contrasts with 'freedom'. Reread the first paragraph of the speech to see how this gives you clues to the possibilities of these words' meanings.

WHY *is this important to her?*

Look at the conflict contained in this scene: her pain at hearing and seeing other women's children; the talk of the eroded cliffs; the double meanings of the 'time to go', the 'life sentence' and her 'freedom'. So this is all of enormous importance to Shirley. It's literally a matter of life and death.

You will appreciate the need to read the whole play when I tell you that the final image the audience is left with just a few seconds after this speech is of the projected words: 'The day she was released from court she committed suicide.'

THETIMEANDTHEPLACE

The play takes place in a 'plain' room which only contains an 'oversized' chair, a bottle of water, a tub of yogurt and an 'oversized' woman's magazine.

No time of day or season are mentioned, the lights just come up to discover Shirley.

Clearly, then, this could be anywhere and nowhere in particular. Are you in her mind?

COM

There are possibilities here for the relationships between Shirley and the audience, herself and her dead child, all of which will form part of the complicity and collaboration between yourself and the panel. It is important, therefore, that you explore your timings when you wish to make the choices concerning these relationships. To begin with, you must decide to whom she is communicating and when this changes.

This speech really will not work if you cannot make the all-important connection to Shirley. If you play the 'attitude' of a woman in grief, or you pretend the 'emotion' of anguish then you will overact and you will not *believe* – so nor will anyone else.

Further exercises

One of the biggest challenges in a speech of this nature is avoiding the sentimentalism trap which can result in melo-dramatic 'gesture-painting' or 'pity poor little me' acting.

'Doing nothing' is a deceptive way of putting it, because it really isn't *nothing*. Rather, it's a very connected truth that empowers you to engage with the scene and character so that you don't have to pile on the 'performance'. Try the following exercises:

- Go through the speech to work out the relationships and the mini-goals in each of its sections.

- Take each section at a time and allow the words to come from the centre of you, with no 'emotion', no funny voice or accent, no gesturing and no facial grimacing; really listen to and think about the words as they come out of your mouth.

- Make a note in the text of anything that strikes you as you do this. Did any phrase stand out for you? How important did the timing become (look at the punctuation and the stage directions)? How important did the weight of individual words become?

- When you have learnt the speech, use someone you know to sit across a table from you and, maintaining as much of the simplicity and clarification as you can, speak to them as Shirley. Note the changes that happen in the way you think about, connect to or make choices about Shirley.

Summary

- Start developing your own working process.
- WWW.THETIMEANDTHEPLACE.COM – make sure you:
  ‣ Know who your character is.
  ‣ Know what they want and why they want it.
  ‣ Locate your scene geographically and in time.
  ‣ Prioritise establishing complicity with the playwright, the panel, etc.

Practical

- Try putting your speeches into your own words.
- 'Hotseat' your characters.
- Thought-track your speeches to discover your running commentary.
- Watch out for 'gesture-painting' or sentimentality in your performances.

7

It Ain't Over…

Auditioning for a place at drama school to train for a career in musical theatre is fundamentally the same as auditioning for acting courses, and you should follow all the advice already given in this book. But there are also some key differences.

Not every actor has to be able to sing, but every musical-theatre performer needs to be able to act. You will probably not have to perform a Shakespeare monologue, but you will have to offer a choice of modern speeches and will be expected to show acting talent and potential here, too.

Choose your speeches in accordance with the guidelines I've suggested for straight acting courses. As a general rule, I would advise against choosing a speech from a musical because they may not be long or complex enough to show your abilities.

Musical-theatre courses

From your research into the schools, you will notice that the performing arts are organic in nature. The thrust of any particular musical-theatre course will depend on the kind of performers that the school wishes to train:

- *Dance as the primary skill*
  Some schools shape their course around performers with excellent dance skills who wish to make these skills the heart of their performance. On these courses the acting and the singing may not carry the same

weight and so you should expect the auditions to concentrate on some challenging dancing.

- *Singing as the primary skill*
  Equally, some performers with outstanding talent in singing will choose a course that allows for maximum training of their voice, and where dancing and acting might play somewhat secondary roles.

- *The 'triple-threat performer'*
  A course purporting to train a 'triple-threat performer' is one that wishes to focus equally on all three skills. Normally, acting is at the heart of the course, which aims to bring all three skills up to a comparable standard. You should expect an audition for a course like this to address each skill carefully, as they're looking for students to train as fully rounded performers.

Making your choice

Begin by looking at your self-appraisal. Are you proficient in all three disciplines? Rank them strongest to weakest to see where you could improve. Have you reached the top grades in ballet and tap, for example, but taken no singing or acting classes? Conversely, have you studied singing or acting for some time but never attempted dance training? Ask your teachers for their opinions and advice to help here.

Having done this, you must now go to each school that offers a serious musical-theatre course, to get the 'feel' of what they do. Watching their graduates in their final show-cases and productions can give you some understanding of the course at the school, and how it might or might not suit you and your skills. And this applies to any production you see, as you note where the actors trained.

Making the grade

There is clearly a place in the profession for excellent dancers and singers. Since the number of males wishing to enter musical theatre is fewer than aspiring female performers, then it must also be said that the chances for outstanding male dancers and singers are even better.

However, it cannot be overemphasised just how high the overall standard is. If you really cannot dance or act very well, for example, or if you are a much better actor than dancer or singer, then you need to be thinking of improving the weak skills – before you get to the audition. Otherwise, if you decide that you really do want to audition for a 'triple-threat' course, then you will undoubtedly suffer by not having at least two of the three skills they will be looking for.

If you feel that your standards of singing and acting are good but your dance is weaker, for example, then check for an option that means the school offers intensive extra work on that skill over the first year – to bring your dance up to standard (this is sometimes called an 'open pathway' option). Above all, you need to be honest with yourself. Don't make excuses for not working on and improving your skills base, because the panel will definitely not be doing so. Use all your time before you audition to prepare.

Your pieces

As well as at least two speeches you will also need at least two good, contrasting songs (see earlier notes regarding the preparation of sheet music). By 'good' in this instance, I mean a programme of songs and speeches that not only shows you to the best advantage in the individual skills, but that complement each other.

And I say 'at least' two speeches and two songs because you should always be prepared to offer alternatives, even if they aren't specified in the audition details. Often, one of the questions of the audition panel on which I sit will be 'If I'd asked you to bring, say, four songs for us to choose from, which others would you have brought, and why?' Indeed, you may then be asked to sing a few bars of whichever song you say – so be prepared!

Choosing your songs

- Don't choose a song just because it's popular – in fact, it's a good idea to avoid anything currently in the West End for this reason (some schools do not even allow this). There is a plethora of excellent musical-theatre solos out there so don't limit yourself by only looking at a few. I wouldn't advise a signature number, either. These are songs that are associated with a particular singer or performer. For example, 'Maybe This Time' from the film version of *Cabaret* (John Kander and Fred Ebb) is strongly associated with Liza Minnelli. You may well be very good at it – but make sure you are before you take the risk.

- Don't choose a song (or a speech) just because you don't think the panel will know it or have heard it before. Choose positively *for you* and you shouldn't go far wrong.

- It's the character singing that makes a song from a musical different from a pop song, so if you are auditioning for musical theatre, then choose a song from a show unless specifically told not to.

- Don't try to second guess what the panel expects, choosing a song just because you think that's what they want to hear, even though it means stretching for that end note (or avoiding it) because it really is out of your range. 'Vanilla Icecream' from *She Loves Me* (Sheldon Harnick and Jerry Bock) is not the song to sing, for example, if you can't produce a good sound in your higher register!

- Choose a song that is appropriate for your age and experience. You must be able to connect with the character and their journey, communicating it with the benefit of your life experience. For example, you might think of choosing 'Missing You (My Bill)' from *The Civil War* (Frank Wildhorn and Jack Murphy), which is a ballad sung by an American Civil War soldier's wife telling of her single-parent struggles as she waits for him to come home. It may be a good song but it's going to be difficult to connect with if you're eighteen and fresh from school in modern Britain.

- A song should tell a story and you are in charge of telling it. Rehearse the song as if it were a speech. You need to make the story jump out clearly and deal with creating the character, and working out your phrasing.

- Songs involve a journey for the character and you must be clear:

  - If the character is trying to make a decision – e.g. 'I'm Gonna Wash That Man Right Outta My Hair' from *South Pacific* (Richard Rodgers and Oscar Hammerstein II).

  - If the character is reacting and changing to circumstance – e.g. 'Losing My Mind' from *Follies* (Stephen Sondheim).

  - If the character is explaining something about their lives – e.g. 'I Wish I Were in Love Again' from *Babes in Arms* (Richard Rodgers and Lorenz Hart).

- In some ways a song can be even harder than a speech because there are also purely physical and vocal elements of technique that must be in place without being obvious to an audience and that the panel will be looking for. For example, 'Summertime' from *Porgy and Bess* (DuBose Heyward and George and Ira Gershwin) needs plenty of good breath support and well-balanced resonance (amongst other things!).

- You might think about choosing a song by a writer like Oscar Hammerstein, Cole Porter, Ira Gershwin or Irving Berlin. They were all masters of the voice in song, demanding every single quality that you would be hoping to bring to a performance in a musical. The panel is on the lookout for all of these. Very often, if you bring a song from a show like *We Will Rock You* (featuring the music of Queen) and offer an alternative song like 'Till There Was You' from *The Music Man* (Meredith Willson) or 'From This Moment On' from *Out of This World* (Cole Porter), an audition panel will ask for the latter, more lyrical number because the range and depth of both the interpretative and vocal qualities demanded will allow them to see your true voice and potential.

Preparing your song

Coming up with a process of preparation is even more individual with a song than a speech, because of the vocal techniques discussed throughout this chapter. Each voice is unique and, if you have one, a singing teacher will be the one to take you through the exercises that are going to help you to excel in audition.

That said, the panel is going to be listening and watching carefully for several elements within a song which include (not exclusively and not necessarily in any specific order) pitch, musicality, and character and story.

- Pitch refers to the centring of your note, so that you hear the note in your head, you prepare your voice and you support the note with your breath.

  Much the same as with dance, you have to be prepared for what is coming up in a phrase of music – in effect, your head has to know where a phrase is going before you actually get there. Hearing it in your head before you get to it stops the syndrome of almost hitting the note and then fine-tuning it. Listen to 'You'd Be So Easy to Love' from *Born to Dance* (Cole Porter) for an example showing how important this is. Your breath support will also join in to help you avoid failing pitching at the end of a phrase.

- The second of the above elements is musicality, and this really refers to your musical sensitivity.

  You have a song to sing which comprises melody and lyrics first of all, so your accuracy in singing what is there in the music of the song is part of your musicality. Then, the interpretative ability and artistry you use to rise to the vocal and musical challenges of the song mean that those demands are met and the song will be honestly and truthfully represented in your performance of it.

  When you are thinking of musicality, think of the tone of your voice and the different sounds you can produce (even on the same note); think of the rhythms and dynamics in your timing; think of your use of the phrasing in a song; think of the resonance in your voice and think of the clarity of the lyrics. All of these (and more) give you your own sound, your 'voice' – and your musicality.

- Finally, character and story. Whilst the musical challenges of a song might make the most demands of you, the journey that the character undertakes in a song must not be ignored. The combination of the actual characteristics of the character you're portraying, the point in their story at which the song comes, and the scene leading into the song all give you clues to the importance and the driving purpose the song plays in the character's life.

An example ('Green Finch and Linnet Bird' from *Sweeney Todd* by Stephen Sondheim; Nick Hern Books)

Sweeney Todd, the barber of Fleet Street, is unjustly convicted of a crime and deported by a judge who wants Todd out of the way so he can seduce Todd's wife and take his daughter (Johanna). With the wife now dead, the Judge plans to marry Johanna and shuts her up in her room inside his house, away from prying eyes.

In Act One Johanna sings this song, 'Green Finch and Linnet Bird', from her window to all the caged birds, when a bird-seller passes by in the street below. In other words, the caged birds are a metaphor for herself. The linnet used to be popular as a caged bird because of its melodious song – and this represents Johanna.

You will have chosen this song because:

- It suits you and your voice – because the song is within your grasp in age and experience, and in range and tone. If you are an alto with a 'blues' tone in your voice then it wouldn't be appropriate, for instance.

- You engage with the emotions in the music and the lyrics – the sadness that plays against Johanna's desire to make the best of the situation, singing even if she cannot fly, like the caged birds.

Now you need to prepare the song. As with your speeches, make sure you understand all the lyrics and that they connect with you deep down. Exactly what makes Johanna start to sing the song? What moment is it that provokes the thought in her that makes her sing? Write out your lyrics as if the song were a monologue in a play.

This will help you to focus on those vital few opening bars with which you will grab the audition panel. All too often a candidate will not know what has happened to the character before this scene or, indeed, what happens to them in the story of the whole musical. Or they may never have even thought of the lyrics as something apart from the music.

Now, as you read those lyrics, trace the journey that Johanna makes in the song. The opening thought gives way to the next and the next – just like the path of thoughts and reactions in a speech.

When you know where you're going in the story of the song you can look at how the musical phrasing works in conjunction with it. For example, is the musical highlight of the phrase the same as the words and sentiment you wish to highlight in the lyrics? In such a good song as this there will always be reasons for the musical phrasing's relationship to the lyrical phrasing.

As with a speech from a play, you must beware 'signposting' what you are doing. Not only is this patronising to your panel, for they will know your song (and may even have performed it in a professional production!), but they are listening to *you* so it's *your* understanding and interpretation they're out to experience. Let them come into what you're doing, don't take all your work out to them, trying to make your interpretation obvious.

You need to be absolutely secure with Johanna's story and the journey you are taking the audience on. You must not undercut your final moments with anything that isn't relevant to the reaction you want to leave the audience with, so recognise the climax of the song and hold that moment at the end – strong and centred in Johanna.

I would definitely not advise 'staging' your number, by which I mean planning dance steps and movements to what you are singing. You will risk feeling foolish because the panel aren't interested in your dance ability at this stage. This doesn't mean standing still like a wooden spoon: natural movement and gesture is fine. But to plan it all out will result in your focus being displaced.

You must show the panel who you are and what you can do, from your choice of the right song for you and your voice, to the techniques you employ to meet the musical challenges of the song, and to the artistry you bring to your interpretation of the character and the lyrics.

Your voice

Your voice is your future, your career and your livelihood. Choose your songs and style with care (and work with your singing teacher, if you have one) to develop the protective techniques that will keep your voice as good as it can be for as long as possible.

When you have trained, you will be expected to perform eight shows a week, so if you 'belt' as a teenager – while your voice is still developing and before you have acquired the technique – you will almost certainly have problems later on in life.

Indeed, an audition panel may well consider that too much damage has already been done for them to offer you a place on the course, so the best thing to do is to avoid challenging songs (such as big rock songs or any song in your 'belt' range) until much later.

Suitable songs

I can't reiterate strongly enough that a song must suit the individual voice and personality of the singer. So you must go through many songs and do your follow-up research when you have decided on your audition choices, to ensure songs that match your range and character.

Here are a few suggestions to start the search for the right songs for you:

Female soprano

- 'The Finer Things' from *Jane Eyre* (Paul Gordon) (This is a showy piece.)
- 'Out of My Dreams' from *Oklahoma!* (Richard Rodgers and Oscar Hammerstein II) (An 'innocent' number with a nice melody.)
- 'Once You Lose Your Heart' from *Me and My Girl* (Noel Gay, Douglas Furber and L. Arthur Rose)(Be careful not to over-sentimentalise this ballad.)
- 'It Might As Well Be Spring' from *State Fair* (Richard Rodgers and Oscar Hammerstein II) (A lovely lyrical number.)

Female mezzo

- 'Someone Like You' from *Jekyll and Hyde* (Frank Wildhorn and Leslie Bricusse) (This is a well-known ballad, so make sure it's absolutely right for you.)
- 'Hello, Young Lovers' from *The King and I* (Richard Rodgers and Oscar Hammerstein II) (If you sing this one, there's every chance you'll be asked to sing your alternative (as well) or scales, since the range is a bit limited.)
- 'Who Will Love Me As I Am?' from *Side Show* (Henry Krieger and Bill Russell) (This is also quite familiar, so make sure it shows off the very best of you and your voice.)
- 'The Light in the Piazza' from the show of the same name (Adam Guettel) (A melodic, flowing ballad.)
- 'Sunday in the Park with George' from the show of the same name (Stephen Sondheim) (This is a funny song, and quite tricky.)

Female alto

- 'The Life of the Party' from *The Wild Party* (Andrew Lippa) (A nice acting number with a build – beware the belting! – but this is sung quite regularly in auditions.)
- 'Hold On' from *The Secret Garden* (Marsha Norman and Lucy Simon) (This song requires a good storytelling personality and you must 'see' the other character.)
- 'Heaven Help My Heart' from *Chess* (Björn Ulvaeus, Benny Andersson and Tim Rice) (This song has some golden notes and a good connection to the audience.)

Male tenor

- 'What More Can I Say?' from *Falsettos* (William Finn) (Beautifully melodious.)
- 'Gigi' from the show of the same name (Alan Jay Lerner and Frederick Loewe) (This song may need cutting, but will show off your voice.)
- 'Beautiful Girl' from *Singin' in the Rain* (Arthur Freed and Nacio Herb Brown) (A lyrical, 'old-fashioned' number.)
- 'All You Can Do is Wait' from *Anne and Gilbert* (Nancy White, Bob Johnston and Jeff Hochhauser) (A lovely lyrical story.)
- 'Proud Lady' from *The Baker's Wife* (Stephen Schwartz) (A love confession song.)
- 'Grand Knowing You' from *She Loves Me* (Sheldon Harnick and Jerry Bock) (A funny and challenging number.)

Male baritone

- 'Make Them Hear You' from *Ragtime* (Lynn Ahrens and Stephen Flaherty) (Serious storytelling is important in this song.)
- 'Be Like the Bluebird' from *Anything Goes* (Cole Porter) (A wickedly funny number.)
- 'It's a Fish' from *The Apple Tree* (Sheldon Harnick and Jerry Bock) (An uptempo, comic number.)

Male bass

- 'If I Can't Love Her' from *Beauty and the Beast* (Alan Menken, Howard Ashman and Tim Rice) (A well-known number from the stage version of the Disney film.)
- 'I Feel Like I'm Not Out of Bed Yet' from *On the Town* (Leonard Bernstein, Betty Comden and Adolph Green) (A warm number requiring good comedic timing.)
- 'Suppertime' from *Little Shop of Horrors* (Howard Menken and Howard Ashman) (A very specific voice is required to sing this – be warned!)

Suitable songs for actors

Remember that a panel for an acting course is not going to judge you specifically on your ability to sing. What they are looking for is someone who can hear a tune, can engage with the character in the song and can put across that character's journey. So, tell the story of the song, no matter how simple it is.

Here are some example songs, which I've heard sung very well, to give you a glimpse of what's out there – but do read the whole of this chapter for suggestions on how to prepare.

Female acting songs

- 'Ac-Cent-Tchu-Ate the Positive' from *Here Come the Waves* (Johnny Mercer and Harold Arlen) (A jazz standard with an up-beat message.)
- 'The Physician' from *Nymph Errant* (Cole Porter) (A comic number with the potential to develop a strong character.)
- 'Speak Low' from *One Touch of Venus* (Ogden Nash and Kurt Weill) (A romantic, lyrical ballad.)
- 'Daddy Wouldn't Buy Me a Bow-Wow' (Joe Tabrar) (A comic, music-hall number.)
- 'The Saga of Jenny' from *Lady in the Dark* (Ira Gershwin and Kurt Weill)(A witty story song.)

Male acting songs

- 'If You Could See Her' from *Cabaret* (John Kander and Fred Ebb) (An exercise in playing against meaning.)
- 'The Joker' from *The Roar of the Greasepaint – The Smell of the Crowd* (Leslie Bricusse and Anthony Newley) (A bittersweet, but uptempo song.)
- 'Fanette' from *Jacques Brel is Alive and Well and Living in Paris* (Jacques Brel, Mort Shuman and Eric Blau) (A sad and nostalgic song.)
- 'I've Got a Lovely Bunch of Coconuts' (Fred Heatherton) (A comic, music-hall number.)
- 'Change Partners' from *Carefree* (Irving Berlin) (Very romantic and lyrical.)

Your dance audition

You may not be asked to dance unless you get through to the recall audition. Unlike the first audition where you'll have free reign with songs and speeches, you will probably have to 'let yourself go' within the choreographed routine set for you.

On occasions, however, if you are recalled you may well be asked to prepare and present your own choreographed section of dance (usually lasting only ninety seconds or so) to give you a freer hand in showing what you can do.

Any dance classes you take, therefore, will help prepare you for your dance audition, either at the preliminary or recall stages. So in advance of this you should look at:

- Correcting your posture.
- Working on the lines and alignments that the panel will look for.
- Making the steps themselves become second nature to you, which will allow you to pick up the routine(s) set. If you have no dance vocabulary, you have to rely completely on unfamiliar visuals to learn both how to do the steps and their place in the routine, and this may make it hard to concentrate and smile at the same time!
- Helping yourself to develop your sense of rhythm, energy and focus in a dance.
- Giving yourself a sense of your own stage presence.
- Helping yourself to formulate your own memorisation techniques that allow you to pick up any routine quickly and accurately – sequentially by movement or words, for example.
- Giving yourself the confidence to listen to the music and interpret it as you pick up the routine instead of developing 'panic deafness'.
- Helping yourself to focus on the spirit of a routine as your technique copes with the actual shape of it – so you won't be left behind.

Summary

- Keep referring to the audition requirements to make sure you're complying.
- Choose your school and course following investigation of approach and content.
- Select your material with regard to what is appropriate for you – would you be cast as that character?

Practical

- Ask teachers and tutors about good singing coaching – learn about your voice and how you use it.
- Attend dance classes so you can develop your technique.
- Investigate acting courses, lessons or books you can read.
- Aim to read as many potential speeches (and the plays they come from) as you can to find the ones that engage you the most and make you feel they were written especially for you.

8
Practice, Practice, Practice

You now know what you are doing, why you are doing it, and how you want to do it, so it's time to look at the elements instrumental in enabling your interpretation to take flight – your voice, articulation and diction, and the exercises that should be part of your working process. Please note that this book does not attempt to take the place of a dedicated vocal workbook (see the Appendix for suggestions), but this chapter will try to get you listening to your body to build an awareness of how it works towards the production of your own unique voice.

Your voice

You must start to observe how you breathe, attach your voice to your breath, resonate your voice, and articulate your words. What follows is a (very) brief starting point for exploration, but your first port of call should be to find a good voice or singing teacher.

Nerves may seem to take over in an audition. Vocal lessons can bring enormous benefit – not only for singing, but to help your speaking voice, too. Nerves will tend to make you speak more quickly and softly, breathe shallowly and tense your neck and shoulders (and any other parts of you that the nerves can attack).

Without going into the technicalities of voice production (again, a matter for your voice teacher), sound is produced by the vibration of air passing through the vocal folds in our throats. It's automatic. But if we try to project (actors should never 'shout') without proper breath support and protection, our throats tense up and damage is done. Tension is one of the actor's worst enemies and breathing properly helps to relax and support the voice.

Your breathing

A vocal coach can take you through exercises to pinpoint any problems specific to you but, in the meantime, try the following exercises to begin your understanding:

- Stand with your head up and your chin level; your knees, shoulders, neck, arms and back relaxed; your weight balanced on your heels and soles.
- Relax your jaw and very gently let your head relax back. Does your mouth fall open? If not, your jaw is tense.
- Breathe in and out normally; note how this feels and what happens in your body.
- Lie down on the floor; breathe in and out, feeling the air fill and then leave your body. What changes do you feel when you breathe out?
- Still lying on the ground, go on breathing in through your nose and then out through your mouth – this time counting to yourself as you do it. How high can you count each time?
- Now imagine that you are blowing your breath out right up to the ceiling – you could imagine trying to keep a feather or a bubble afloat. Be careful to remain relaxed through this and don't try to strain to do more than you can.

Never attempt this for more than a few moments at a time. All you're doing is trying to identify the way you actually breathe and to see how your mind and imagination is attached to what your body is doing.

Using your breath with your voice

- Repeat the first exercise, again imagining that your breath is reaching up out of you from the centre of your body.
- This time, as you try to 'breathe' the feather to the ceiling, go through the vowel sounds (you can start with a hum and open the sound out into the vowels, if you like).
- Keep checking to make sure there's no tension in your body. Does it feel different when your voice is coming out on the breath?

Your resonance

If you try to speak while your neck and throat muscles are tense, you will find that the sound you produce will be (unpleasantly) different from the sound you make when you are relaxed. This is because the vibrations can't properly bounce around freely the way they can when you're relaxed.

This bouncing quality is called 'resonance' and it affects the tone of your voice. There is a good, rich depth to your voice when the resonance is balanced, and this will help you when you want to build the flexibility in your voice.

Your chest, your face (including your nose and mouth) and your neck are all the areas that vibrate, and to make the most of the resonance, you need them all to be relaxed. Try the following to identify the feeling of opening your throat:

- Stand in front of a mirror and drop your jaw open very gently.
- Breathe in through your mouth and feel the 'open' feeling at the back of the throat.
- Close your mouth slowly and gently without closing the back of your throat.

- Hum very, very softly (don't strain at all) – can you feel what happens in your throat when you do this?

All you are doing here is beginning to connect with what's happening in your own body, so you are aware of the different sounds you can make when your voice is working with a good balance of resonance. It's important, because your voice is the magic instrument that communicates everything you sing and say.

Your articulation

Articulation is all about how we shape our words using what are called 'articulative organs'. These include your throat, the roof of your mouth and the area behind this (which is touched when you say 'k', for example). You also use your tongue, lips, teeth (and the little ridge just behind your upper-front teeth).

Articulation can be drastically affected by accents and the important thing to remember is that actors must be able to get rid of any 'baggage' in the way they speak normally, so that they are able to find another accent, for example. Trying to adopt one accent without first going through a neutral received pronunciation (RP) will mean you carry all your original vowel shapes and sounds with you. Instead of an accurate accent and good articulation, you can end up with an uncomfortable-sounding hybrid accent (a strange mid-Atlantic drawl of half-American and half-English is one such blend).

Also, the way that you form your words (the consonants specifically) can affect how you convey the meaning of a song or speech. For example, if the 'r', 's', 'f', 'v' and 'th' are badly affected, it might cause an audition panel to suggest you go away and work for a year to smooth out the problems before applying again. It makes sense, then, to be aware of any problems at the outset and before you arrive for that important audition. Here are some tips for spotting potential concerns and what to do about them:

'R' sound

An 'r' sound is made when the tip of your tongue curls back to touch behind your upper-front teeth, with the side rims touching the upper-side teeth. But problems occur if you use your upper-front teeth and the inside of your lower lip to make the sound. In this case, you need to get used to making the sound by curling the tip of your tongue back.

- Say 'sh' – what position is your tongue in?
- Say 'sh' and let your mouth fall open without moving your tongue (in effect, this almost sounds like 'er').
- Now keep that sound going into 'oo', curling the tip of your tongue behind your upper-front teeth as you do it.
- Practise this movement until you can hear a clear 'r' sound.
- Practise tongue-twisters:
  - (er)Raise the (er)Roof.
  - B(er)ring th(er)ree t(er)ucks (er)round to the (er)rea(er)r.

'S' sound

An 's' sound is made by the strong, middle part of your tongue (the blade) and the sides touching the upper-side teeth gently. The air is sent down the centre of the tongue – it shouldn't escape at the sides. Nor should the tongue tightly push against the roof of your mouth and teeth or the sound will become sharp (in extremes it can even sound like an 'f'). Try to relax your tongue shape to allow the air to help the sound formation.

- Practise saying 't' with the tip of your tongue bouncing off the teeth as strongly as it can (as in 'Tommy').
- Now make the tongue bounce very weakly off this ridge, so that it sounds 'watery' in quality (in effect, a sound not dissimilar to the 's' sound).
- Make the 't' sound sustaining it into the 'watery s' and then into all the vowel sounds.
- Practise this, using all the vowels, until you can make the 's' sound securely.
- Now practise saying the vowel sounds into the 's' sound.
- Practise tongue-twisters:
  - (t)So many (t)sick (t)sycophantic (t)snake(t)s.

'F', 'v' and 'th' sounds

Sometimes there can be problems with distinguishing these sounds; for example, when an 'f' or 'v' is substituted for 'th' (as in 'thing' or 'this' becoming 'fing' or 'vis'). An acting student must guard against this in normal speech or in dialogue (unless you're choosing to adopt it for a character).

If you have difficulty distinguishing between the use of these sounds then you may need to seek the help of a voice teacher.

- Say the 'th' sound (i.e. as in 'thing') using the tip of the tongue gently touching the upper-front teeth.
- Say the 'th' sound (i.e. as in 'this') with the tongue in the same position, but vocalising the sound more.
- Practise these sounds in different sentences and tongue-twisters, until you are confidently using the right consonant and sound in the right place without having to think about it:
  - Thirty-three thirsty, thundering thoroughbreds.

- Form the 'f' sound using the upper-front teeth making gentle contact with the outer, lower lip and say the sound as you read some text or recite some tongue-twisters:
  - ▸ Four furious friends fought for the phone.
- Form the 'v' sound by adding in the voice to the above sound.

'G' and 'k' sounds at the end of words

Other sounds that you need to be aware of are the 'g' and 'k' sounds at the end of words. A common problem is the glottal sound of 'g' being substituted for the silent 'ng' and this can be due to accent as well as habit. You need to practise keeping your epiglottis in the raised position (the rising feeling at the back of your throat) and then letting it sink down gently and silently.

- Let your mouth fall open and say 'ing'. Can you feel something rising at the back of your mouth? That's your epiglottis.
- Let the word finish but keep your epiglottis in the raised position.
- Now trying letting your epiglottis fall silently.
- Say 'ing' again, making sure that there is no sound at all when the epiglottis falls at the end.

The key thing is to always listen to your voice objectively. Record yourself reading a newspaper article, then listen to it play back, making notes. Don't record your audition speeches because you may start to listen to the 'acting' and not the vocal qualities. Don't be overly alarmed if you hear things you really don't like – if you start in good time and work hard then there's time to correct most faults before your audition.

Your body

A preliminary audition for actors will not specifically show up any problems you might have with your physicality – unless you are required to participate in a dance or movement workshop.

If you are a musical-theatre candidate, you need to check your audition information to see the details of your preliminary audition, but it's likely that dance and movement will play a more crucial part.

Even if you will not be assessed predominantly on your physical or movement skills, it does not mean that you can forget about them, because you should at least have:

- Good knowledge of your overall fitness and stamina. This is where your gym work comes in – or even the sport you play at school.
- Awareness of your suppleness and strength. Dance classes will do much to help you with this.
- Movement coordination and the ability to take in information, process it and put it into action (for example, simple movement routines). Again, dance classes will do much to help with this.

Posture problems will make themselves evident in any audition and, since these can sometimes add to vocal problems, you should be aware of them and take steps to correct them. If this is the case, a course in the Alexander Technique, for example (see the Appendix), may prove invaluable. Indeed, a drama school may ask you to complete a course such as this, as a condition of taking up any place they may offer you.

Final preparations

It's important that, once you've reached this stage in your preparations, you are rehearsing your speeches and songs with specific goals in mind, as opposed to simply running through them again and again until they're mechanistic and fixed with inflexible decisions.

What this means is that you must find 'the moment' each time you rehearse or perform, so you don't lose the spontaneity that will engage an audience (the panel!) in what you are doing. It also means keeping yourself open to the different acting choices that various imaginative exercises can suggest.

What follows are some further exercises to help you see how you can keep your programme fresh and spontaneous as you build up to the audition itself.

Use just one exercise at a time, keeping its specific goal in mind and making sure you note down any new ideas or sensations that open up your connection to your character and their situation.

Your senses

As an actor, all five of your senses should be constantly alert and attuned to the world around you. Studying each sense, one by one, will help you centre yourself as a performer; working through them whilst imagining what your character experiences and feels in the same circumstances will provide a helpful way for you to see the world through their eyes, and how their perception differs from your own.

- Sight
  - Stand and look around the room you're in. Really *see* it objectively and examine every little detail of it and the things in it.

▸ Walk around the room. Then crawl around it to get a different perspective. What would your character see?

• Touch

▸ Blindfold yourself and feel your way around the room. Touch everything, noting the different textures, and testing how cold or warm things are.

▸ Repeat the exercise – but this time try to experience it as your character would. How would they react to touch in your scene or song?

• Smell

▸ Again using the blindfold, register the different smells in the room – of the dust, of the curtains, of a coffee cup, etc.

▸ Repeat the exercise as your character. What can they smell and what is their response?

• Taste

▸ Try tasting lots of different foods, especially those you might not have tried before.

▸ Again, repeat this in character – what sense would the different tastes make to your character? How do they respond to what they do and don't like?

• Hearing

▸ Lying down, listen to the sounds outside the room; then to those inside the room; and finally inside your own body. How difficult did you find this and how did it affect your concentration?

▸ Now try to make sense of the sounds as your character would. How much easier or more difficult was this?

Your physicality

- Try your speech or song using different kinds of movement, noting the effects on your character and especially to see how it alters the meaning of what you're doing or saying:

  ‣ Swaying from side to side, then from heels to toes.

  ‣ Jumping up and down quite gently then progressively more energetically.

  ‣ Moving around the room in flip-flops.

  ‣ Moving around the room in very high heels or very tight shoes.

- Imagine you're performing your speech or song while walking barefoot over a variety of surfaces, again noting how these different surfaces force you to move differently and make subtle (or not so subtle) changes to your physical characterisation:

  ‣ Walking over sharp pebbles or shingle.

  ‣ Stepping on hot tarmac.

  ‣ Wading through water up to your knees.

  ‣ Crossing a river that's frozen over... you think!

- Try doing something else while you rehearse your speech or song, even if the activities don't have anything to do with the context of your pieces. See how doing these alters the subtext for your character and, as a result, the meaning of what they're saying:

  ‣ Counting dried peas or sweets.

  ‣ Tying your shoelaces or tie.

  ‣ Putting on your make-up without a mirror.

  ‣ Writing out your shopping list.

Your choices

There are various exercises that can help you to explore the timing and phrasing within your speech, thereby opening up the possibilities of your acting choices so you can be spontaneous and open on the day of your audition:

- Work through your piece, writing in all the thoughts and reactions between the lines to help you understand the progression of the journey your character makes and how one thought leads to another.

- Speak your speech or song in gibberish, so you can focus on how your choices are (or are not) interpreting the meaning of the piece.

- Deliberately change the phrasing pattern of your speech or song to see what is changed. Does it help you to understand why the writer has chosen the words, sequences and rhythms they have, for example?

- Set a metronome ticking and explore different tempos for your piece; this is harder if you're working on a song, of course. How does a tempo alteration affect the meaning? Can you operate one metronome tempo for your thoughts and another for your external movements, for example?

- Rehearse your speech or song using different subtexts to explore the strength of your chosen subtext. So try it:
  - As gossip in a library.
  - As an apology you actually mean.
  - As an apology you don't mean.
  - As if it were a comic stand-up routine.
  - As if it were an argument waiting to happen.

- Explore how different deliveries can alter the meaning and objective in your speech or song by changing your motivation. Try the following statements, or other relevant examples, underlying your piece:

> ‣ 'I saw what you were doing.'
> ‣ 'Don't you try to stop me.'
> ‣ 'I just heard someone trying the door.'

- Try different, unexpected actions for each thought and moment in your speech or song. These should be expressed as transitive (active) verbs that you *do* to the person you are talking/singing to (or yourself if it's a soliloquoy or solo song):

> ‣ 'I punch you.'
> ‣ 'I caress you.'
> ‣ 'I threaten you.'
> ‣ 'I seduce you.'
> ‣ 'I provoke you.'
> ‣ 'I amuse you.'

- Play your scene for the opposites in it – for example, play your tragedy as if it were a comedy, or the comic speech as if it's full of pathos or self-pity.

What these exercises will help you to do is to explore all the many options you have open to you. Some things won't work at all, but that will help you realise what *does* work. Maybe something will help you develop the complexities you need to demonstrate in your audition, and make you open to the possibilities in your audition programme, both as you prepare and on the audition day itself. Ultimately, these exercises will build your understanding of your character and their situation. Without losing any of the 'living in the moment' quality which you must retain, you can reach a point of knowledge and understanding that will give you momentum in your audition.

Summary

- Begin to familiarise yourself with your own voice and speech patterns, and work on the areas that need development.
- Read and absorb at least one vocal-technique workbook to help you, or get a vocal/singing coach to work with you.

Practical

- Formulate your own exercise and rehearsal regime starting with these exercises to explore all the possibilities in your speech or song, and in conjunction with your chosen workbook (and, if you have them, teachers and/or coaches).

66 The biggest shock of starting my training was giving myself completely to the school, realising that it is the most important thing in my life – and having to be 100% disciplined at any given time!

Georgia (BA Acting, LAMDA)

9

On the Day

The day has finally dawned and you have arrived early at the audition (at least half an hour before you are called) so that you give yourself time to warm up and focus. Even if the drama school has timetabled a full warm-up you need to go through your own routine to channel your energy and focus on the task in hand.

What to wear

A word is needed here about dressing for auditions. You should not try to make a strong connection between fashion and your personality – do not wear heavy make-up or clothes that reveal midriffs, knicker elastic or any flesh that might cause the panel discomfort. It's you they want to see, not a department store's make-up counter and window displays. Equally, avoid the trap of thinking that a dramatic, gelled and spiked hairdo will show you off better. This isn't the kind of eccentricity they're looking for.

For the same reasons, leave any big, rattling and distracting jewellery at home, especially any piercings. This is particularly the case with tongue piercings which will both affect your speech and wind up whoever is auditioning you! Avoid teetering in on skyscraper heels; be prepared to be asked to go barefoot if you are auditioning in a dance studio with an expensive floor and you're wearing stilettos! These are all weapons of mass distraction and will not help you in the audition room. You will almost certainly feel vulnerable in there, but you should trust the panel to respect and warm to that vulnerability.

With all the above in mind, choose comfortable clothes and shoes that do not take the attention away from the bare canvas of you. Neutral, light make-up means your eyes can convey your personality more powerfully. How you dress should enable the panel to focus without the distraction, embarrassment or irritation of a fashion statement.

Your surroundings

An early arrival also gives you time to perform another important task: taking in the atmosphere of the place, and observing your surroundings and the people who will be looking after you (usually current students roped in to help with the auditions).

You can learn a great deal from this observation period, particularly from these students. How relaxed and happy to be there are they? How friendly and willing to help you relax? They will give you a good idea of what studying at the school is like and should be happy to answer any questions you might have (ask them one thing they like about the school and one thing they don't, for example).

Focus, focus, focus

After the warm-up (either conducted on your own or as a group) is an important time, too. You need to sit quietly to relax and focus while waiting to be called into the audition room. Try not to chat too much with other people when it's approaching your audition time, because this can dissipate energy and concentration and, somewhat ironically, it can also raise the panic levels in a kind of 'mass hysteria' effect.

You can begin to play unhelpful 'comparison games' in your head if you aren't focused on yourself. For example, 'She looks like the kind of person they'd want here' or 'Why on earth didn't I choose the speech he's doing?' You are here because of *you*, and you are as valid as anyone else. Stop the second-guessing right now – you do not know the specifics of what the panel is looking for in you, for their course or on that day, so just focus on yourself and what you want from this day, so you can give of your very best.

Your entrance

You may be auditioning in a fairly small room or (hopefully) a larger room with good light. Your focus must be absolute since your audition might not take place with silence all around. Other auditions and/or classes may be in adjacent rooms, and if current students or teachers are allowed to enter and view auditions, you must be able to focus without being distracted. Distraction will mean you forget your lines and dry, which is a sure sign that you were not in the character and the moment.

You must be aware that you are being auditioned from the moment you set foot into the room. Your entrance must clearly show the real *you* so, given the importance of these first thirty seconds, leave your bags and coat outside the room. If this isn't possible, carry them in unobtrusively and leave them just inside the door, so the focus is on you and not them. (But do remember to take over your music and/or pieces as needed.)

Don't enter like a tornado, chattering and acting manically, and don't slither in like someone who wishes they were almost anywhere else. Look at each person on the panel in turn, making eye contact with each of them and shaking hands (if this is appropriate). Smile and introduce yourself in an assured, positive manner (or just say 'Hello' if the person showing you in has introduced you already).

You are making the impression of a focused, professional person who takes the audition seriously but with anticipation. You are in your element. You are at home here.

It may be appropriate here to mention the ubiquitous water bottle. Constant swigging from the bottle can be a rather disconcerting and distracting habit. By all means ensure that you are hydrated – but something may be very wrong if you are needing to swallow water every few seconds, and cold water may not be the best thing for your vocal cords at that moment. Try to put yourself in the panel's position and to see yourself through their eyes. Maybe you could just leave the bottle with your coat and bag for the short time the audition takes?

Your interview

As discussed earlier, it is possible that the panel will not talk to you until after your performance. It is perfectly possible that they will not talk to you at all, which can be off-putting, but don't let it affect you one way or another.

Let's assume they do ask you a few questions – many do to help relax you, as well as giving them time to take some initial notes. Remember that nerves can affect behaviour as well as voice. Do you clam up when you're nervous? Or do you 'gush', not letting anyone else get a word in? Do you wave your arms about and laugh noisily? Panels are very experienced people and they can see through much of this to what they are looking for in this preliminary audition, namely:

- The appropriate physical and vocal qualities and potential (i.e. appropriate for their school as well as the business).
- A positive, centred attitude.
- The right kind of self-assured personality (bearing in mind that 'self-assured' does not just mean 'loud').

Already, your entrance to the audition has gone some way to preparing the ground and arousing their interest in you.

You must be specific, and also be ready to answer the more obvious questions like:

- Why do you want to act?
- What plays have you seen recently and what did you think of them (musical-theatre students should include plays as well as musicals)?
- Do you have any favourite composers or playwrights?
- Why do you want to come to this particular school?
- Why do you want to study on this course (including an awareness of what you need to improve as far as your technique goes)? Be as specific as you can.
- What do you feel you have to offer as an actor?
- Where do you see yourself in five years' time?
- What would you do if you couldn't become an actor?

These questions may take slightly different forms but your preparation will have put you in a good position to answer them in any framework without resorting to 'Because I want to be famous' or 'Because I want this more than anything'.

Just listen carefully to what is being said to you and try not to worry. Let your quiet confidence continue as you talk about yourself, about the things you have achieved and those you want to achieve.

Asking questions

Because you will have done your research about the school and the course, you will be able to ask the panel interested and intelligent questions about the course. You should also be able to make good comments about what is pertinent about the approach at this school and why it suits you (for example, this may be a course favouring the 'triple-threat performer').

You should also be able to back up any comments or questions you make by reference to a third-year student showcase or production you saw. Just knowing that you can talk about all of this, should they ask, will give you confidence and should soothe frayed nerves.

Don't try to be a clown and don't try to impress by being 'cool' or arguing with what the panel says. Trust them, they know what it's like to audition and they want you to give the best you can of yourself. Remember, they will want to make your audition as positive an experience as possible.

Your performance

It's all come down to these few minutes. This is your audition and you are in control of it. You have prepared, worked and focused on this moment for a long time, so:

- Introduce your speech choice(s) clearly and carefully – play, playwright and character. Don't mumble or gabble.

- Know which speech or song you'd rather do first, as the panel may choose which they want to see or they may ask you to make the choice.

- In the case of musical-theatre auditions, the panel may sometimes require singing first or they might leave it to you, so think about how you would like to do it before you go in. It also makes sense to remember the reasons for choosing each of the speeches and songs in your programme. For example, 'This character resonated with me because…' or 'I identify with his or her background.' Alternatively, 'This character has my sense of humour and I really understand where he or she is coming from.' Be aware that they will probably then ask what you mean!

- Have clean copies of your speeches on the table where the panel can see them, but don't be worried if they don't look at them because it's rare that you will be performing a piece with which they are not familiar (they may have heard it already that day).

- Have faith in yourself – don't rehearse drying in your mind!

- Stand approximately two thirds of the way back in the space between the panel and the wall behind you. This is your acting space.

- Take a moment before you begin to focus and reconnect with the character and what's happening in the scene. This also establishes for yourself (and the panel) exactly where any other character in the scene is on the stage with you; if you can see him or her then so will they.

- Do not visualise any other onstage character at or on the panel's table unless you are told to do so. Equally, if the character is speaking to the audience for any reason, do not look directly at the panel members and/or act to them if they haven't specifically required you to do this. Unless a panellist (or current student who's helping) wishes to stand in for the other character, the panel do not exist in your character's world. So it is psychological torture for them to have to make notes about someone who is talking directly to them (particularly if it's strong subject matter). Moreover, since they are not characters in your performance, their reactions will be the reactions of someone who is very seriously concentrating on everything you as the actor are doing in the here and now. Your brain will read these reactions as negative or positive comments on your acting and this can subconsciously pull you out of character and concentration.

- If you're addressing an audience in your speech or song, deliver the lines to an 'audience' above the panel's heads. A particular line *might* be delivered to the panel to make a point, but never the entire piece. Believe in what you are performing and the panel will not exist.

- Don't be thrown if a panel member stops you before the end of your speech and starts to give you notes or direction. This means that they want to see a different interpretation, they want to see how well you can respond to notes, or something's getting in the way and they want to help. Listen carefully to them and accept whatever changes they make to your acting choices. Take the opportunity as they have presented it to you – they want to see if you can take their direction and be flexible and open, or if you have fixed your choices. This can be an indicator of interest in you, but whether they're interested or not don't let it affect you beyond listening and responding to what they say. Definitely do not argue with them!

- When you finish your speech, hold the moment before relaxing back into yourself and breaking out of character.

- Take the panel's guidance as to what you must do next. They may want the next speech or to rework something in the first speech, maybe standing in for the other character. They may talk to you now if they haven't already. Alternatively, they may just say they'll be in touch (and this does not necessarily mean an automatic rejection).

- If, God forbid, you do dry for some reason, don't panic and step out of character. Don't apologise or ask what you should do. Instead, say nothing, remain in character, lower your eyes slowly towards the floor while breathing out to release the tension and clear the brain. Trust me, if you have done your preparation the words will come back. The panel may not say anything at all during this time, but they will be watching you like hawks to see how you deal with the situation. You must not let forgetting your line throw you completely; an audition is not simply a memory test. It doesn't feel or look good if you forget your lines, but the panel will know why – and you are human (thank goodness!). If you fall apart completely, just ask to start again. Put the first run out of your mind, take your moment, breathe, focus and start from the beginning. The sheer thought of this happening should spur you to preparing as thoroughly as you can!

Throughout your audition you must remember that the panel *want* you to be what they are looking for, and they know just how frightening the experience of an audition can be, so they will treat you with respect and empathy. If they don't, then perhaps this is not the place for you. It is your choice as well.

When you've finished your pieces and had your chat/ interview with the panel, you should gather your things together, smile and thank the panel (again making eye contact with each of them). Only shake hands if it seems appropriate (they may offer theirs, for example). Then you should leave with the same dignity that you entered.

Recalls

Following a successful preliminary audition you will be recalled to be considered even more seriously as a possible member of a drama school course.

This recalling may take place on the same day or over one or several days at a later date, but will include any (or all) of the following:

- Your speeches worked again – perhaps with the course director, or deconstructed and reformatted (as part of a duologue improvisation, for example).
- Your song(s), again worked in more depth or perhaps only a certain number of bars.

- An additional component, perhaps a sonnet that forms the heart of a vocal workshop, or a third contrasting speech.
- An acting workshop, exploring a different genre of plays, for example.
- A dance workshop/routine (to check physicality, fitness and aptitude to receive and act upon information given).
- An improvisation workshop.
- A sight-reading exercise.
- A more in-depth interview or question-and-answer session, perhaps with the school principal or course director.

The recall panel will usually differ from the preliminary audition panel, since you'll have more workshops to participate in. There may be a greater number of the school's tutors present, including the director of the course and, possibly, a director from the theatre business or a professional company member. The principal of the drama school might also be there if there is an interview or question-and-answer session.

The workshops will be taken by professionals, members of staff (who might also be in the business), and they will be observed by a panel. Alternatively, there may be a rota of workshops and panels with each of them taking notes from their specialist point of view.

Be prepared for the recalls to take place with all the prospective candidates present and working together (in some cases, several of the current school students might also be in the room). Don't panic or let your nerves get the better of you. The situation is the same for everyone.

Even more than they did at the preliminary audition, the panel will be assessing your ability to work as a team member. This doesn't mean you must 'put on an act', which can happen if you react to the sometimes very public nature of the recalls. On the contrary, too much 'standing out from the crowd' nearly always leads to the panel thinking that you are an attention-seeker and, therefore, *not* a good team member. Even worse, they may think you are not a student who is seriously committed to the work in hand. Have the confidence to focus on what you do best; that's what you're here for.

Instead, the panel and the workshop leaders are looking for a candidate who:

- Engages with the character, scene and context.
- Possesses raw talent and shows the greatest potential from the training point of view of that particular school.
- Demonstrates a professional standard of knowledge of their pieces (including why they could be cast as their characters); the background to the plays and musicals their speeches and songs come from; the place in the world of theatre that these plays and musicals hold.
- Communicates and uses initiative in ideas with a spontaneous and sensitive response to a conversation or situation.
- Can willingly take direction and imaginatively explore their work in different directions, even if these are completely surprising to them.
- Shows a sense of humour that is generous to others and responsive to the situation.
- Is able to process the information received.
- Above all, listens.

Your speeches

Very often (and even if it happened in the preliminary audition) the director of the course will want to work one of your scenes with you to see if you are able to take direction and brave enough to make different acting choices.

It cannot be too strongly emphasised that, in order to take advantage of this opportunity to demonstrate your hunger and ability, you must know these pieces so well that you do not have to think about the words. As you take the 'risks' that are asked of you, it is what you are doing that you need to be thinking about, allowing the words to come from the centre of you and be expressed spontaneously, without a voice in your head screaming, 'What do I say next?'

Of course you may dry on something if the approach is radically different from how you imagined and rehearsed it before, but a director will know the difference between drying on your lines arising from trying some completely new idea or resulting from lack of preparation. And it's your attitude to embracing the challenges that can make the difference. Good preparation will do much to alleviate the stress and surprise of what is asked of you.

You may also have to use your speech as part of a duologue situation with another candidate. In effect, this may be as simple as bouncing lines off each other, or it may demand that you and your partner make sense of some of the lines from your individual speeches, constructing a completely new situation and 'conversation'. The panel might expect you to develop an improvisation around the circumstances of the speech. If this happens, clearly you must go with this fresh situation.

I do not advise 'mugging' with misplaced comedy or inappropriate overacting to cover feelings of self-consciousness. You can only respond to a new approach if you are immersed in it and totally focused. Never feel embarrassed – everyone in the room is doing or has done the same thing.

And remember that you really can't second-guess the panel and will not be able to see in their eyes exactly what they're looking for!

Your songs

As with your speeches, you may well find yourself singing to the other candidates at your recall, as well as to the panel.

Along with the speeches, you should aim to be so comfortable with what you are doing that you are not thrown by the situation. Let the song's journey guide you and not the situation (so no 'sending it up' for the new audience and other students, for example). The integrity of what you are doing must come first at all times – it will save you when other elements may not be so kind.

You will undoubtedly hear others singing, and some candidates will allow self-doubt to undermine them as they listen to what they assume is so much better than their own performance. It might be, but it probably isn't. You've won your place in this recall just as much as they have. So enjoy what they do, certainly, but don't use it to pick apart your confidence – or to allow you to become complacent.

Whether you are aiming for a place on an acting course or a musical-theatre course, this is what the panel is watching for. Do your preparation so you can take your opportunities and enjoy them.

Extra speeches and songs

Having spent time carefully selecting pieces with specific reasons behind your choices, choosing an extra speech should not pose problems for you. Try to contrast the material in style, period or character type to your other pieces, but always keep the 'connection' rule in mind (and keep referring to the brief of the school).

If you have to prepare a sonnet for your recall audition, then you need to think about the imagery and the language. Speak it from the heart, using the simplicity which befits such a beautiful example of poetry. Avoid a 'cod-Shakespearian' delivery where you play the attitude instead of the emotion. Let them hear *you* in your voice.

Again, working on a new sonnet might take place with the school's voice coach, and you may be given the sonnet a day or two before (depending on when the recall audition is). Alternatively, you may know that it's required from the preliminary audition pack you were sent, and you could think about it in advance.

Movement workshops for acting courses

A movement workshop during your recall audition may take the form of an imaginative movement pattern or physical 'story' to which you must react and respond, or a very fast and energetic routine of moves and patterns.

This isn't to highlight your technique as a dancer so much as your fitness, coordination and ability to understand what you're told, and then put that information into action. Your energy, enthusiasm and commitment are all important here.

Being puce in the face, worryingly out of breath and obviously struggling to understand the task will all speak volumes to a panel who knows just how tough the course is. Equally, someone who loses their temper or is desperately copping out of doing the moves doesn't show themselves in a good light.

Not only that, but your concentration will be disrupted by being out of condition or in a temper. You must be agile enough to undertake whatever is thrown at you, no matter what your level of physical fitness. Actors come in all shapes and sizes and you will probably not be surrounded by would-be models. However, you will be expected to be physically and mentally up to the course. Again, your ability to receive and process information will also improve with your preparation – as will your fitness, so it's best to get on with some sort of movement classes if you suspect your dance and physical fitness lack something.

Dance workshops for musical-theatre courses

There is going to be a difference in expectation (and content) between a musical-theatre dance workshop and a movement workshop for a more traditional acting course. For musical-theatre auditions, be prepared to participate in a routine that will be enough to show the panel exactly how much knowledge and technique you have. A dance workshop might run as follows:

- A warm-up.
- Your own prepared movement.
- A ballet class with routine.
- A jazz or modern routine.
- Possibly another routine of modern, less formal dance to show personality as well as technique.
- You may be asked to attend a further dance class (particularly if the panel are considering you for any open pathway route where you will get intensive training on your weaker skills).

There is no hiding place when you perform a routine, unfortunately. Either you can pick it up or you can't, and either you have the technique to connect with it or you haven't. However, both of these elements can be improved upon, as your pre-audition dance classes will show you, so don't wait until you've applied to a school to improve what you can do. Assume that everyone at the audition will be of a high standard and start working now!

But you must also remember that you are not going to be patronised and given some overly simplified dance routine at your audition. The panel is looking to see where you could be taken on the course, so, again, do not try to second-guess what they are thinking. Trying your best and doing 'just well enough' can be sufficient.

There are also other, more subtle, things that the panel will be looking for whilst you are stretching, counting and carrying out your barre and corner work, etc.:

- Are you focused or are you busy noting what everyone else is doing? Or checking to see if the panel spotted that you didn't make that last pirouette?
- Are you enjoying what you're doing or do you have a look of complete panic on your face?
- How do you react to getting a step wrong? Do you laugh and try to make everyone else laugh because you can't do it? Or do you react with even stronger concentration so you get it right the next time?
- Are you trying to hide at the back all the time?

It doesn't take a genius to tell what a panel would rather see, but at any rate, you must definitely not be paying more attention to what the panel is thinking than to what *you* are supposed to be doing!

Improvisation workshops

If you're applying for an acting course, it is probable that you will be asked to improvise at the recall audition – on your own, with a partner or in a group. For example, you may be asked to participate in a 'corporate-bonding' improvisation where you must all improvise solving some problem or other. Alternatively, in another improvisation example, you might be asked to imagine going for a walk in an ornamental garden, having to keep to 'paths' along which others will also be walking.

Again, the panel is looking for the qualities you display while under this different kind of pressure. Think about how you act in these situations in advance.

- Individually or with another candidate:
    - ▸ Do you convey your sense of enjoyment of working like this?
    - ▸ Do you respond freely and imaginatively to what's being said to you?
    - ▸ Are your ideas based on what will make other people laugh or on what comes from the situation given?
    - ▸ Do you seem to be out of your depth with this form of work or able to go with the moment?
    - ▸ Do you listen carefully to what's being said to you or do you interrupt halfway through?
    - ▸ Do you seem to want to catch the panel's eye rather than engage with your ideas?
- In a group:
    - ▸ Do you take charge of the situation and try to shape everyone else's improvisation to fit your ideas?
    - ▸ Do you allow yourself to be pushed into doing something you are either not comfortable with or don't understand fully?
    - ▸ Do you listen to everyone's ideas and contribute your own with sensitivity?

Students of Drama and Theatre Studies at school will be au fait with improvisation work and will not be thrown by these 'what if' situations (sometimes their challenge lies in not dominating the situation). However, you can still prepare yourself even if you have not done so much improvising before. Try the following:

- Look through the questions above and think about what your approach and attitude could and should be in those situations.

- Practise picking up an object and telling a story about it; for example, a personal object (like a pen); an impersonal object (like a wastepaper bin); an item of clothing (like a shoe); a book.
- Draw up a list of memories that cause you to react in some way: tasting something you hated (or loved); crying at a film; thinking of something that made you spontaneously laugh, etc.
- Improvise various situations that might lead into (and out of) your speeches or songs.

Improvisation comes from a freedom of imagination so focus and relax. It should also be fun!

Sight-reading

On very rare occasions, you may be asked to read something that you've not prepared. Here are a few hints that may help you:

- The panel will not want a fluent, precise, speedy and glib reading of the words on the page. You are going to train as an actor, and actors don't go on stage and read. What they're after is your interpretative response to what you are reading.
- If you've been told nothing about the piece, ask what has happened before the scene begins.
- If the panel want an instant response (they may not give you time to read it through to yourself beforehand), they will not judge you because you fluff the lines.
- Go with whatever jumps out at you while you're reading the piece. There will be clues. For example, lots of punctuation might mean the character is excited, angry or upset; short lines can mean firmness or could mean someone who's shy or unwilling to talk for some reason.

- Remember to go from moment to moment and see where it takes you.
- Read more slowly than you would normally act – take your time, don't put on a funny voice or accent, just feel your way through it as yourself.
- Think of pauses as pearls, so the more you give away the fewer you have (i.e. don't overplay them).
- Keep the ends of the lines open so your voice freely responds to the piece; for example, don't use a flat monotone or repeat downwards inflections to 'resolve' each line.

Your recall interview

This may be your first real chance to talk to any of the recall panel. Look back at the advice on first-round audition interviews earlier in this chapter. Remember that you must show confidence, not arrogance; intelligent knowledge of the art form and yourself (including your strengths and weaknesses); and a hunger and passion to learn and improve. Know and be able to justify why this specific school will be able to help you do all this.

Summary
- Arrive early; enter assuredly; interview intelligently; perform professionally.
- At a recall, communicate potential, sensitivity, generosity, humour and commitment.

Practical
- Consider your list of personal attributes. What skills can you improve upon? What can you do on your own and where do you need the drama school's help? Use what you've learnt of each school and its philosophy to help you to think through why and specifically how each drama school can help you.

66 I had no idea when I was in the sixth form that I needed to do so much to prepare for the audition rounds, so I needed pushing. But once I started to audition seriously, it paid off. It wasn't just that I got my brain in gear as an actor, but because I'd done so much work, my audition pieces were part of me and I was confident enough to do whatever they asked me to without being thrown by any of it, and to show them who I was. I ended up really enjoying the auditions. I'm sure it's because of that that I had several offers to choose from, including the one that I really wanted and I felt completely ready to start my training.

Jack (BA Acting, Drama Centre)

The Final Word

When it's good news

So, you've done your research and preparation; you've come to know a bit more of what you are like and what your ambitions are; you've investigated all your funding options and are confident that the requirements are (or will be) met to help you on your way. You've chosen the school you want to attend; you've worked hard for your audition and performed well in it; and you've been offered a place! Congratulations!

But what next? What do you do in the intervening months between your offer (and acceptance!) and taking up that place in the new academic year?

Now is the time to put all the practicalities in place and to continue those good habits of curiosity and observation.

The practicalities

Tedious though it might be, you must ensure that all your funding applications and arrangements are in place. The last thing you want is for a last-minute hiccup to throw a spanner in the works.

If this is the first time you have left home, then you must also not underestimate the effects of beginning what will be a very tiring (and sometimes emotional) experience in your life. So make sure that you get on with any accommodation needs as soon as you can. Your first step is to approach your drama school and take advantage of whatever help they can offer you, from recommendations of accommodation agencies, or lists of current and new students seeking flatmates. These tend to be snapped up quickly, so there's no time like the present!

The school will also provide you with a list of required clothing and reading. You may be able to find some second-hand books or rehearsal outfits (skirts, footwear, etc.) – again, ask the school.

Hopefully, by the time you get to this point, you will have developed habits that will stand you in good stead at drama school and beyond. Look at your world with the eyes of one who will observe and examine human psychology, behaviour and condition for some time to come. Continue to attend the theatre and cinema, art galleries and museums. Continue to drink in life. There is no need to become some kind of expert before you begin to train, for your school is waiting to show you the next steps.

When it's not such good news

Let us address your panic at this point. You should not regard a 'failure' at a single preliminary audition as some final indication of your ability. Each drama school is different, and all are looking for their 'type' of student. It's true that continued rejection from all the schools you have chosen could be said to be a warning that you might have to address some issue or other and, if this does happen, carefully work through all the stages covered in this book to see whether you can develop any specific area.

Quite a few people need to do more preparation work than others and take a bit longer to get to the required level – it is not the end of the world if this is you. However, continued lack of success does mean that you need to look at your goals, your skills and any disparity between what you are offering and what the schools want, so that you can make the right decision for you.

It is unlikely that you will be able to appeal a panel's decision unless they have made errors in the way that the audition was run or in the administrative criteria used to determine your suitability for the course, for example.

If the panel feel that you were 'borderline' and that you might be able to progress yourself to a stage where they would offer you a place, they may advise you to concentrate on something specific before reapplying – dance or singing classes, for example. However, even this may not happen and you should not rely on receiving feedback.

Your future

No one who knows anything at all about acting or the profession would tell you it's easy. Forging a career as an actor demands dedication, hard work and commitment way before 'talent' (that most difficult to explain element). It's a craft.

The most famous, the most highly thought-of (and the most highly paid) actors would be frightened of calling it 'easy', in case they offended the character who plays a big part in any success – Lady Luck. For you can do everything that everyone tells you and *still* face desperate times and rejections. Personal opinions of audiences, directors, other actors, playwrights – and drama schools – dictate a great deal in the profession. But this doesn't mean that your opinion is worth less than anyone else's.

As I said at the beginning of this book, if you do your preparation work you can vastly enhance your chances of success. Nevertheless, it might not be the right time for you at the moment. You may need to develop your skills base a bit more or maybe you need to clarify your own ideas of what you want to do. You will have to think clearly and positively about what you could have done differently, and sometimes you will know quite definitely what went wrong.

But you also need to remember that not everyone who has trained at the school of their choice succeeded at their first time of auditioning. Indeed, many students needed that extra time before they were in the right place at the right time. So do not give up at the first hurdle. You will know when the right time comes for you to consider other options in life. And one round of rejections is definitely *not* that time.

If you do have to go back to the drawing board, keep your eyes and ears open – and work, work, work on your skills base. Aim for the best (in yourself, your training and your career), be tough and honest when you have to be, but also patient and caring towards yourself as you would be with a good friend. Then next year…? It's all to play for.

The very best of luck to you.

❝ I was so tense and worried that if I didn't get in it would be the end of the world. I didn't – and it wasn't. I took a year's foundation course and it was a very positive experience. Because the course was only for a year, I focused on who I would be as an actor, not just a drama student. At my second attempt I relaxed and enjoyed the auditions because I knew more about myself and what I wanted – and I got a place. If you want to be a musical-theatre actor you really need to be honest with yourself – don't use a strong discipline as a comfort blanket – work on the other skills.

Mary (Foundation Course, LAMDA; BA Musical Theatre, GSA Conservatoire)

A Postscript for Parents and Teachers

It is always difficult in this ever-changing world to give definitive advice to a young person wanting to pursue a career in acting. When that young person also happens to be your son, daughter or student it can be nigh on impossible.

For parents

It is never easy to strike the right balance between guiding and encouraging your son or daughter on the one hand, and pushing and persuasion on the other. But in my experience – as both a teacher and a parent – the first port of call must be the drama school professionals who are well aware of the industry needs and of the quality of students they wish to audition and train.

Be guided also by the hunger, talent and personality of your child. They will need determination, dedication and discipline. They will also need a clear head, clear sightedness and a thick skin. And they will need to possess their very own brand of talent that will set them apart from others.

It is this last quality that so often brings, if not disaster, at least avoidable heartache, for there is nothing worse than witnessing the rejection of someone you care about. It is a fact of life in the arts that, whatever you do and whatever success you achieve with it, everyone will face rejection at various points along the line. To be rejected at the very beginning because you are not in the right place yet, however, is very painful. It's an uphill struggle to turn someone into an actor when they don't want to be one, or to turn someone away from it when they do! So be absolutely sure that this is the profession your child is dead-set on entering. Be vigilant that their desire is for the right reasons, and heading in the right direction. Be encouraging but be judicious. Don't let your encouragement become pushing or shoving; let your child develop in their own way. I've heard someone say on an audition panel, 'I sometimes feel it's the parents we should be auditioning!'

If your child is determined, then all you can – and must – do is to support, support and support. They will need you to be there for them – but be guided by them in exactly what their needs are. In the beginning, at least, they will need to do a lot of preparation to build their skills base and to get to know exactly what is going to be expected of them – at audition and beyond.

For teachers

It can be enormously gratifying when a student asks for advice on going into the performing arts. The help you can offer will make all the difference between success and failure at the audition stage. Their preparation is vital, and guidance in choosing and rehearsing their material is paramount.

It's important to recognise that drama schools do not want to see a finished article as far as the actor goes – why would they be there to train? Nor are they unduly concerned with seeing a lot of 'acting' going on. What they want is for a young talent with a sense of purpose in what they're there for, a knowledge of and passion for the pieces they have chosen, and a realistic sense about their prospects of being cast in those roles.

Speaking as someone who auditions hopeful students, the joy of seeing someone engaging with their character and the text is great. It's improved upon by hearing them speak about the profession they wish to enter with an informed enthusiasm. As their teacher, you know them, you know their strengths and weaknesses as potential candidates for the drama schools – they're lucky to have you there to guide them and support them.

In conclusion, the one thing that seems to me to be a constant in these changing times is the absolute privilege it is to have a vocation in the arts. It is both a burden and a blessing. Tough, yes. Sometimes heartbreaking, no question. But undoubtedly worth it.

Appendices

Drama Schools, Funding and Contacts

There are many drama schools and courses of all types, but the ones on the following non-exhaustive list of drama schools have a certain standing in the profession and are as fit as any for the purpose of training a professional actor. A small sample of each school's alumni is also listed to give a sense of who has trained there.

I have not included any schools that do not offer BA Acting courses or who have changed their courses away from specialist acting (at the time of writing). Many of these schools also offer a variety of other courses specialising in different areas.

You need to keep up to date with the drama schools that are changing their courses and offering new courses all the time – including foundation courses, part-time skills-enhancement programmes or collaborative ventures in preparation for full-time training, for example.

Looking at the websites will show you the variety of schools and their approaches to training the modern actor. Be open-minded with 'audition-training' courses because they can each take on the characteristics of the school's approach – which may or may not suit every individual. Remember, too, that the only way to test a school's appropriateness for you is to research their prospectus and website, see their graduate showcases, and attend an open day there.

Academy of Live and Recorded Arts (ALRA)
Jimmy Akingbola, Sarah Parish, Hannah Waddingham
www.alra.co.uk

Arts Educational Schools London (ArtsEd)
Julie Andrews, Will Young, Catherine Zeta-Jones
www.artsed.co.uk

Bristol Old Vic Theatre School
Daniel Day-Lewis, Naomie Harris, Pete Postlethwaite
www.oldvic.ac.uk

Drama Centre London
Paul Bettany, Anne-Marie Duff, Colin Firth
www.arts.ac.uk

East 15 Acting School
Stephen Daldry, Alison Steadman, April de Angelis
www.east15.ac.uk

Guildford School of Acting
Michael Ball, Brenda Blethyn, Tom Chambers
www.gsauk.org

Guildhall School of Music and Drama
Eileen Atkins, Orlando Bloom, Ewan McGregor
www.gsmd.ac.uk

Italia Conti Academy of Theatre Arts
Claire Goose, Ben James-Ellis, Claire Sweeney
www.italiaconti.com

The Liverpool Institute for Performing Arts (LIPA)
Lindsay McKenzie, Dawn Porter, Sandi Thom
www.lipa.ac.uk

London Academy of Music and Dramatic Art (LAMDA)
Benedict Cumberbatch, Anna Maxwell Martin,
David Oyelowo
www.lamda.ac.uk

Manchester School of Theatre
Steve Coogan, Julie Walters, Victoria Wood
www.theatre.mmu.ac.uk

Mountview Academy of Theatre Arts
Eke Chukwu, Amanda Holden, Ken Stott
www.mountview.org.uk

Oxford School of Drama
Babou Ceesay, Claire Foy, Kiran Sonia Sawar
www.oxforddrama.ac.uk

Rose Bruford College
Ray Fearon, Gillian Kearney, Gary Oldman
www.bruford.ac.uk

Royal Academy of Dramatic Art (RADA)
Gemma Arterton, Ralph Fiennes, Ben Whishaw
www.rada.org

Royal Birmingham Conservatoire
Rebecca McQuillan, Jimi Mistry, Catherine Tyldesley
www.bcu.ac.uk/conservatoire/acting

Royal Central School of Speech and Drama
Judi Dench, James Nesbitt, Jennifer Saunders
www.cssd.ac.uk

The Royal Conservatoire of Scotland
John Hannah, James McAvoy, David Tennant
www.rcs.ac.uk

Royal Welsh College of Music and Drama
Aneurin Barnard, Rob Brydon, Dougray Scott
www.rwcmd.ac.uk

The important thing is that you apply for the schools you feel are right for you and will provide what you want from your training, bearing in mind that each drama school does have its own approach and philosophy. I cannot overstress the importance of researching each school thoroughly, not only so you will reduce the chance of making a mistake and feeling like a square peg in a round hole, but also so that you can enhance your chances of being offered a place when you audition.

By the time you have finished all your preparation work, you will have a good idea of yourself and what you want. Then, when you attend an open day, part-time course, exam or graduate showcase in a school, you will have a good feeling about where you are most at home. All of this isn't infallible, but you will have done as much as you possibly can to avoid making a mistake, so you can go with your instincts if you are offered a place.

Funding

The options and 'goalposts' of paying for drama school training change all the time; so much so that this book deliberately doesn't go into too much detail – as it's all liable to change. However, one thing is consistent: you can be sure that it will cost a lot of money, often tens of thousands of pounds. For this reason, you should begin the process of familiarising yourself with all possibilities in parallel with your training research and keep yourself up to date with all the changes. Whilst it's important to be realistic and aware of the challenges involved, don't let financial concerns prevent you from considering going to drama school. Increasingly, many schools will work hard to help talented students from lower-income backgrounds to attend.

Do not wait until you have applied, auditioned and succeeded at your audition before thoroughly investigating how you will be funded throughout your course. It is important to understand as quickly as possible what you are up against in terms of the amount that you will need, so that you keep abreast of all the government funding rules and initiatives that may give you additional support.

Whether you qualify for government funding depends on several things – including the drama school you are applying to and the course. Some loans and grants are means-tested, so are based on personal or family income. You may be eligible to apply for a low-interest Career

Development Loan. If you already have a degree, you won't be eligible for any further maintenance loans.

Many schools themselves offer bursaries and/or scholarships, which you should investigate. As you are researching the establishment that is the best 'fit' for you, the details of their ability to help you apply for financial assistance will become clear. It is always possible to appeal to other organisations and/or individuals for contributions towards your funding costs, and many students obtain small sponsorship amounts from many people and businesses. You may even be able to secure some kind of sponsorship from a high-profile institution like a football club, as in one instance I know of. It might take much ingenuity, creativity and perseverance but it can be worth the effort.

Here are some websites which will give current advice on student funding.

Government Student Finance www.gov.uk/student-finance
This website will keep you up to date with all of the legislation, the key differences between loans, grants and bursaries – and full information on how to apply.

National Union of Students www.nus.org.uk
The NUS is an organisation which looks out for the interests of all students. Their website offers advice on all aspects of being a student and provides answers to many of the questions you will have about funding.

Dance and Drama Awards (DaDA)
www.gov.uk/dance-drama-awards
There is useful information on the DaDA website and which explains the intricacies of this type of award, the private institutions where they are available, the amount of award you might expect, and the instances in which a decision regarding the award may be appealed.

Other useful contacts

Contacts
Contacts is a book of names and addresses that is invaluable for any actor; it contains everything from agents to venues, photographers to drama schools and is available annually from Spotlight (see below, www.spotlight.com/shop) or from good bookshops.

Spotlight www.spotlight.com
Established in 1927, Spotlight is arguably the original casting service used by directors and casting agents. Among other things, it is a publication of actors' photographs and details (in book form and now on the website). The company also owns spaces in London which are sometimes used for auditions.

Equity www.equity.org.uk
Equity is the trade union for actors and professional performers, covering all the entertainment industry. The union fights for pay deals and also offers legal support and advice on your acting career and contracts, etc. As a member, there are also discounts on various things such as subscriptions and products, and they have a special student membership rate.

Useful websites

The following organisations are all mentioned in the book:

Alexander Technique www.stat.org.uk

Amateur Theatre Network www.amdram.co.uk

Association of Teachers of Singing www.aotos.co.uk

International Dance Teachers Association
www.idta.co.uk

Little Theatre Guild www.littletheatreguild.org

National Youth Music Theatre www.nymt.org.uk

National Youth Theatre www.nyt.org.uk

Masterclass at the Theatre Royal Haymarket
www.masterclass.org.uk

Music Teachers www.musicteachers.co.uk

Old Vic Theatre www.oldvictheatre.com

The Questors www.questors.org.uk

Royal Exchange Theatre www.royalexchange.co.uk

TAG Theatre Company www.citz.co.uk

Suggested Reading List

Ignorance is the curse of God
Knowledge the wing wherewith we fly to heaven

William Shakespeare, *Henry VI, Part Two*

There are many 'theory' books on the market that will point you in various directions. Some of them will engage you, others may not. To avoid huge initial expense, explore your local library and also second-hand bookshops (and websites like Amazon Marketplace or Abebooks). Your tutors will have recommendations and may even have lending copies in the school or department library. You must learn to ask, and ask to learn!

Below are a few suggestions that might help you on your quest for knowledge (and which would all make excellent Christmas or birthday presents!). Choose whichever you feel most helps you start to clarify the mystifying process of acting.

Theatre and theatre history

A Dictionary of Theatre Anthropology: The Secret Art of the Performer
(Eugenio Barba and Nicola Savarese; Routledge)
The hardest thing can sometimes be to connect your understanding of the art form to what a performer is actually doing (with all the nuances of energy and physicality). This book will open your eyes to many performance elements that you may not have thought about before. A gem to dip into.

The Art of the Actor
(Jean Benedetti; Methuen Drama)
Jean Benedetti traces acting from ancient times to the present in a wonderfully accessible and interesting way, using his own clear-sighted explanations and the words of philosophers and writers including Gogol, Diderot, Copeau and Artaud. There's much food for thought here on what acting means and what has shaped that meaning for us.

The Theatre: A Concise History
(Phyllis Hartnoll and Enoch Brater; Thames and Hudson)
The evolution of theatre through the ages to the modern day, this book is a wonderful historical reference book for actors interested in their art form.

Different Every Night – Freeing the Actor
(Mike Alfreds; Nick Hern Books)
Mike Alfreds is an immensely experienced and respected director who brings all of his experience to bear in this book about the relationship between actor and director, that special collaboration. With passion and wisdom he painstakingly explains his techniques of preparation and application, using clear examples and tips.

Approaches to acting

The Complete Stanislavsky Toolkit
(Bella Merlin; Nick Hern Books)
At some point in your training (probably sooner rather than later), you will work on various aspects of Stanislavsky's system. Bella Merlin has taken the writings of this founding father of actor training, redefining and illustrating his ideas into clear, demystified examples which will develop your understanding of training, rehearsal and performance through Stanislavsky's eyes.

Respect for Acting
(Uta Hagen; John Wiley & Sons)
Uta Hagen was a highly respected and talented actor who dissects what it means to use yourself in acting. With honesty and warmth she helps you to develop your knowledge of how you use your skills and senses, explains exercises to encourage discipline and sense of truth, and then shows you how to explore the approach to a role. Her love and respect for the art form is infectious.

The Actor and the Target
(Declan Donnellan; Nick Hern Books)
Using the extremely useful tool of a fictitious actor (Irina), Declan Donnellan wrestles with the mysteries and dichotomies of acting and theatre to help the actor become 'unblocked'. A renowned director, he explores the nature of an organic art form in a hugely practical and insightful book.

Actions: The Actors' Thesaurus
(Marina Caldarone and Maggie Lloyd-Williams;
Nick Hern Books)
This is an invaluable book for actors. To act is to be active, and opening up the imagination to all the possible actions you can play can sometimes be difficult. This book offers many definitions of actions that will help the process.

The voice and the body

Awareness Through Movement
(Moshe Feldenkrais; HarperCollins)
If you have never really thought about your body or the ways in which you move, then this is a wonderful book to begin the journey.

Laban for All
(Jean Newlove and John Dalby; Nick Hern Books)
Rudolf Laban was a dancer and choreographer who believed in the desire and power in all of us to dance and

move expressively. This book is a good introduction to his work and principles, which are taught in many drama schools.

Finding Your Voice
(Barbara Houseman; Nick Hern Books)
Make no mistake about it, if you want to improve your voice you will need to put in the work – and this can be a bewildering task. Barbara Houseman's book explains in clear terms the ways in which you can discover your personal voice and how to use it, but with a sense of humour that puts the 'fun' into functional, no matter how much or how little voice work you've done before.

Assignments in Musical Theatre: Acting and Directing
(Jacque Wheeler, Haller Laughlin and William-Alan Landes; Players Press)
This book is crammed with excellent advice and practical exercises to help the budding musical-theatre actor learn how to analyse songs and characters and how to formulate an organic working process. It even includes assignment sheets which you and your singing tutor can use (though these aren't necessary for understanding what the book is explaining). It's both enjoyable and informative.

The Singing Voice: An Owner's Manual
(Pat Wilson; Nick Hern Books)
This is a very clear, very helpful book on the craft of singing that really makes vocal work interesting. From picking your material for auditions to keeping in shape to sing, Pat Wilson will inform and entertain you.

Monologue collections

Remember the 'health warnings' and use these collections to begin your working process, not replace it! All monologue compilations are very popular ports of call for students and are performed often.

National Youth Theatre Monologues: 75 Speeches for Auditions (Edited by Michael Bryher; Nick Hern Books)
This expansive volume contains seventy-five monologues for male and female actors, all taken from plays performed by the NYT, by writers such as Zawe Ashton, Moira Buffini, Carol Ann Duffy, Brian Friel, James Graham, Dennis Kelly, Rebecca Lenkiewicz, Gbolahan Obisesan, Evan Placey and Jack Thorne. Also included are tips on performing the speeches from current and former NYT members, plus advice on preparing for auditions.

The Good Audition Guides (Nick Hern Books)
Each volume in this series features speeches from a range of well-known and less expected plays, all prefaced with detailed information about the speech, including suggested ways to approach it:

Audition Songs
Edited by Paul Harvard

Classical Monologues
Edited by Marina Caldarone

Contemporary Monologues
Contemporary Monologues for Teenagers
Edited by Trilby James

Shakespeare Monologues
Shakespeare Monologues for Young Men/Women
Edited by Luke Dixon

Methuen Monologue Books
Methuen Drama's extensive range of monologue and duologue books contains the following titles:

Classical Monologues for Men
Classical Monologues for Women
The Methuen Book of Modern Monologues for Men

The Methuen Book of Modern Monologues for Women
The Methuen Book of Contemporary Monologues for Men
The Methuen Book of Contemporary Monologues
     for Women
Edited by Chrys Salt

The Methuen Book of Monologues for Young Actors
Edited by Anne Harvey

Audition Speeches for Young Actors 16+
Audition Speeches for 6–16 Year Olds
Edited by Jean Marlow

Theatre biography

Other People's Shoes: Thoughts on Acting
(Harriet Walter; Nick Hern Books)
This is a very warm, human and immensely accessible take
on an actor's life. It contains many insights into the work
and also into the personality of an actor.

Being an Actor
(Simon Callow; Vintage)
Another hugely entertaining and informative book through
the eyes of one of our great raconteurs.

Complete Works of Shakespeare
(Jonathan Bate and Eric Rasmussen; Macmillan)
This book represents a fresh version of the First Folios of
Shakespeare's works. It contains not only the plays, but
accessible notes and introductions.

Glossary of Terms

The following words are not necessarily technical or literary terms, but a list of words to help you understand the basics of what people might say to you at your audition. They're mainly to prevent you from feeling lost or more stupid than anyone else (which you are not) if a request is fired at you.

ACTION   What you physically do. An action is what a scene needs to 'work', and is often described in terms of something you do *to* another character.

AD-LIB   To make something up if you forget your lines – be cautious here as this is not something usually advisable and tutors tend not to look kindly on it (unless in improvisation).

ALEXANDER TECHNIQUE   A physical technique which helps posture and alignment of the head, neck and back to strengthen and free up breathing, and release the voice (among other things).

ASIDE   Words spoken (usually to the audience) that the other characters cannot hear (see CONVENTION below).

BEAT   A momentary pause.

BLOCKING   The basic movements of the character as determined by playwright, director and actor.

BODY LANGUAGE   When feelings and thoughts are indicated by movements, gestures or posture.

BOMBASTIC   Where the language is too emotional and 'big' or inflated for the occasion (for example, Falstaff in Shakespeare's *Henry IV* plays).

CENTRING   The process of focusing and channelling the heightened state into your work.

CHOICE   The decision made by an actor or a director as to the interpretation of a character.

CLICHÉ   A mannerism or way of doing things that has been done before (till all originality is lost).

CONVENTION   When the audience accepts something you do onstage as real, even though it is only real in an artistic sense (for example, the stage itself is only pretending to be another location, or the other actors only pretending not to hear an ASIDE).

DECLAMATION   A loud, emotional statement.

DOUBLE-TAKE   An exaggerated, (usually) two-stage response to another's words or actions, used for comic effect.

DRAMATIC IRONY   When the audience is aware of something that one (or more) of the characters is not.

DRY   When you forget your lines.

GENRE   The 'family' that a play belongs to – for example, a musical, a comedy, a tragedy, etc. There are also sub-genres like absurd comedy or black comedy. (See following section on Theatre Genres for more notes.)

GIMMICK   Something you might do or a voice you might use to get the audience's attention.

GIVEN CIRCUMSTANCES   All the information you find in the text when you're creating a character. Your given circumstances include the context, personal details of a character, and any other clues you can find.

HAMMY   An over-the-top acting style or way of speaking that conveys nothing of the truth of the situation; sometimes (rightly or wrongly) referred to as 'am-dram' (referring to amateur dramatics). If someone says this to you, they mean you to go back to your centre of truth (and your thoughts and reactions).

IAMBIC PENTAMETER   A verse form (particularly common in Shakespeare and classics) consisting of unstressed and stressed 'feet' in a line – di-dum di-dum di-dum di-dum di-dum.

IMPROVISING   Responding spontaneously to create another scene or situation off the cuff. It's very good for freeing up actors and for understanding difficult passages in rehearsal. Don't use it to 'show off' in auditions – stick like glue to the truth.

INFLECTIONS   These (usually) affect the ends of lines – if you ask a question then the end of the line goes up, for example, but if you bark an order, then the inflection can go down. The aim is to have a flexible, free voice that has varied tone and inflection. If you listen to the way in which you speak when you act and hear repeated inflections, go back to your thought-path and start again.

INTERPRETATION   What an actor and director decide is the meaning in a character or play (and how they decide they will play it comes from this).

LIVING IN THE MOMENT   Responding to what happens right at that moment and reacting spontaneously – so that this seems to be the first time you've said or done these things, and not thinking about what you're going to say or do next.

LYRICS   The words of a song.

MAKING IT BIGGER   A direction to make the delivery less subtle and more energetic. It can apply to movements and gestures or to vocal delivery – it doesn't just mean ditching the truth, though!

MANNERED   When you use the same gesture, facial expression, phrasing or vocal habit again and again instead of finding a means of expression arising from the moment.

(TO) MARK   To run something through to commit what you do to memory and/or to perfect the action/dance steps before performing with one-hundred-per-cent commitment.

(TO) MASK   To block another actor being seen by the audience.

MUGGING   Upstaging another actor by using exaggerated facial expressions (i.e. removed from your centre of truth so you are not LIVING IN THE MOMENT). In the audition scene this can sometimes mean making faces at the people who are not in the scene to cover your own embarrassment.

PACE   The speed of a speech or play.

PARAPHRASE   To be inaccurate with, or condense the lines so that you only get a general drift of what the character is saying.

PARODY   A piece that imitates another in exaggerated style in order to make fun of it.

POSITIONS ON THE STAGE   If your play is set on a proscenium arch (or end-on) stage then downstage is always nearest the audience; stage right and stage left are always from the point of view of the actor; upstage is always furthest away from the audience. If you are playing 'in the round' when the audience is all around you, then you can use the face of a clock or a compass as a reference for the BLOCKING.

PRESENCE   The way an actor commands attention on stage (without UPSTAGING).

SATIRE   A piece that aims to highlight an aspect of a person or society in order to make fun of it.

TRIPLE-THREAT   This refers to a musical-theatre performer who is equally strong in the three disciplines of acting, singing and dancing.

TYPECASTING   When a role is given to you just because of the way you look or behave, sometimes repeatedly.

UPSTAGING   When you do something to take the audience's attention away from another actor (for instance, MUGGING).

Theatre Genres

Students of Drama, Theatre or Performance Studies will have a good understanding of different genres of theatre and of the various practitioners who have influenced theatre. The main thing is that you have a working idea of the period, style and genre of your chosen material and of historical and contemporary practitioners that affect the playing of your characters and the sense of the scene. A panel will expect a certain amount of awareness of the elements that will have shaped your acting choices. For one thing, it demonstrates your interest in your craft.

Indeed, it will help you to discuss your engagement with the characters and your playing decisions – especially when you come to recall auditions. Here are some brief summaries of theatre genres and styles between the sixteenth and nineteenth centuries, with which you may not be familiar. It's certainly not all you need to know but offers a basic background for you to think about, some ideas for areas you might want to research yourself, and a starting point if you are preparing a speech from one of these periods.

Commedia dell'Arte

Commedia dell'Arte was a style of acting in Italy in the sixteenth-century, characterised by big, bold acting, stock characters and physical comedy. We can see the remnants today in Punch and Judy shows, as well as influences of this style of mainly improvised acting in the work of writers like Ken Campbell or Dario Fo. Think of Keystone Kops or Charlie Chaplin – it's that big and clear.

Elizabethan and Jacobean

The Elizabethan period in drama was so called because Elizabeth I was on the throne (1558–1603), and the Jacobean period followed (1603–25) being in the reign of James I of England (and VI of Scotland). Of course, the dominant playwright (and arguably the best) of this time was William Shakespeare.

The plays of this time were written in a mixture of prose and verse (iambic pentameter or blank verse is the main form you may have heard of, but there are others). As an actor, you need to be very aware of when the writing changes from one of these to another, since the changes will give you many opportunities in your acting. The plays were staged without the fussy sets we can have nowadays, and contain very little in the way of stage directions – so you need to look at the speeches themselves for clues about time of day, the character's mood or the general atmosphere of the scene.

Even though you might feel that plays from this period need some kind of special 'voice', try to avoid it. Go through the piece and make sense of it in your own words, then go back to the text and allow your new understanding of the language to guide you. One helpful thing might be to annotate your script with the points at which the character you are speaking to changes their focus; for example, when Hamlet stops talking to himself and turns his attention to another character or to God. You don't need to use a funny voice or mannered delivery.

Other writers to consider from this period are Ben Jonson, Thomas Dekker, John Webster and Christopher Marlowe (to name but a few). It can also be useful to look at the work of Shakespeare or his contemporaries if you're preparing a highly stylised piece (like a character from a Steven Berkoff play, for example).

Restoration Comedy

When Charles I was beheaded (and his son, Charles II, fled to France), the interregnum (when plays and theatres were suppressed) began in England. The Restoration is the name given to the restoration of Charles II to the throne in 1660. Not only did he restore the monarchy to the country, he brought with him a completely different kind of play from those that were being performed when he left.

Restoration comedies caused a great rumpus with the Puritans – not least because it was the first time women had been allowed onstage. At the heart of the plays were sex, money, reputation and status – and how to get more of them! The language is like verbal champagne, fizzing with wit and rude jokes. And since Charles II was fond of dancing, the movement was graceful and elegant. If you get the chance to play in a Restoration comedy, you can really relish the asides and repartee of the characters.

Have a look at George Etherege, William Wycherley, William Congreve and John Vanbrugh. Whilst you may not be performing a Restoration piece at your audition, if you choose a monologue from a modern play like Stephen Jeffreys' *The Libertine*, you will need the contextual help of the original style. Studying the style of this genre will also help in the preparation of other pieces, such as the plays of Oscar Wilde.

Eighteenth-century sentimentalism

Of course, all that fun couldn't go on for ever without people taking exception to the subject matter and bawdiness. As the eighteenth century went on, the criticism (mainly religious) started to mount up, and the plays were expected to have some kind of conscience.

In response to this, playwrights started to put more 'emotion' (or sentiment) into their plays – characters could no longer get away scot-free with their foolishness.

At this time, we can also identify the (very small) seeds of what would grow into a strong movement later on. Denis Diderot (1713–84) was a French philosopher who wanted to see a bit more 'reality' on the stage and he could be said to have put forward the idea of a 'fourth wall' – the imaginary barrier that closed off the stage which the audience 'looked through', rather than having the characters presented directly to them. It wasn't quite the work of Stanislavsky yet, but certainly a tiny step in that direction.

George Farquhar is a good example of a playwright who contributed to both the Restoration and the more sentimental style of the eighteenth century. Other playwrights to consider are Richard Brinsley Sheridan and Oliver Goldsmith (although this will really only affect you in your audition if you choose a modern piece with style origins in this period).

Realism and Naturalism

In 1859, Charles Darwin's *On the Origin of the Species by Means of Natural Selection* threw a whole new idea into the melting pot. He put forward the theory that, as individuals, we behave as we do because of our heredity and environment – our genes and the way we were brought up.

The way that this manifested in the theatre was that writers started to see their characters as real people, who lived lives that the audience could (and should) relate to. This meant that they had to be much more 'believable' than previously – although perhaps not entirely 'real' in style, as we would consider it today.

Henrik Ibsen and Anton Chekhov both wrote plays that probed deeper levels in terms of characterisation – but these were still beautiful plays that had room in them for symbolism and imagination.

Constantin Stanislavsky (1863–1938)

Most students of Theatre Studies will have done some kind of work on the principles of this man. A wealthy Russian actor and director, Stanislavsky is regarded by some as the father of our modern-day realistic acting style. Annoyed by the undisciplined acting of his day, that took no real account of the depths to which he felt an actor should go, Stanislavsky was really the first to formalise some kind of theory of acting.

The exercises that an actor was to carry out – both on himself and on any role he was to play – are still taught today throughout the world. He believed, essentially, that if an actor was to be a true artist, then he would have to draw on his own emotions and his own subconscious. This would allow him to avoid making the mistakes of using clichés on stage.

Actors can use the system of exercises to help them when they come up against a problem in rehearsal and every student should at least be familiar with the books the Stanislavsky wrote (particularly *An Actor Prepares*) to explain his system. Most drama schools will have one or more of these on their reading list.

Bertolt Brecht (1898–1956)

Bertolt Brecht was a German writer and director who really believed that the power of the theatre should be used to achieve something more than just entertaining people. He wanted the audience to have a good time as well, but he felt that you should be able to experience a show intellectually and objectively so that you might just relate to it enough to go out of the theatre and change your society for the better.

A tall order for a play, perhaps – and you can see that a realistic style of acting, where an audience can relate to the characters and lose their objectivity, would not be any good here. Brecht had his actors narrate the story, sing songs and talk directly *to* the audience – and even sit onstage throughout the performance in order to make it clear that they were just actors and not the characters. In this way, that fourth wall is well and truly broken. This is, as he called it, *epic* theatre.

www.nickhernbooks.co.uk

facebook.com/nickhernbooks

twitter.com/nickhernbooks